PENGUIN

BY

DESIGN

Wherever you go-take a Penguin Book

Penguins, taken on the train
Elevate and entertain
Pelicans, as you'd expect
Suit the adult intellect
Puffins, on the other hand
For the growing mind are planned

Poster designed by William Grimmond (20 × 30 inches).

Phil Baines

PENGUIN

BY

DESIGN

A Cover Story 1935–2005

PENGUIN BOOKS

For Jackie, another Penguin book

PENGUIN BOOKS

Published by the Penguin Group
Penguin Group (USA) Inc., 375 Hudson Street, New York, New York 10014, USA
Penguin Books Ltd, 80 Strand, London WC2R ORL, England
Penguin Group (Canada), 10 Alcorn Avenue, Toronto, Ontario, Canada M4V 3B2
(a division of Pearson Penguin Canada Inc.)
Penguin Ireland, 25 St Stephen's Green, Dublin 2, Ireland (a division of Penguin Books Ltd)
Penguin Group (Australia), 250 Camberwell Road,
Camberwell, Victoria 3124, Australia (a division of Pearson Australia Group Pty Ltd)
Penguin Books India Pvt Ltd, 11 Community Centre,
Panchsheel Park, New Delhi – 110 017, India
Penguin Group (NZ), cnr Airborne and Rosedale Roads, Albany,
Auckland 1310, New Zealand (a division of Pearson New Zealand Ltd)
Penguin Books (South Africa) (Pty) Ltd, 24 Sturdee Avenue,
Rosebank 2196, South Africa

Penguin Books Ltd, Registered Offices: 80 Strand, London WC2R ORL, England

www.penguin.com

First published 2005
8

Copyright © Phil Baines, 2005

The moral right of the author has been asserted

Set in Adobe Sabon and Monotype Gill Sans Display Bold
Designed by David Pearson
Colour reproduction by Dot Gradations Ltd, Wickford, Essex
Printed in China by Hung Hing

ISBN: 0–14–102423–2

Contents

Introduction

With a tiny number of notable exceptions – Anthony Burgess's *A Clockwork Orange*, for example, or John Berger's *Ways of Seeing* – very few paperback book covers have the same relationship with their contents as pop record sleeves have with theirs. This is mainly because the first mass-market paperbacks were reprints of existing titles licensed from hardback publishers, and any visual association with those books' previous existence was unwanted. As paperbacks evolved, so did ideas of how they should appear and how they should reach their intended market.

Penguin books, first published in 1935, were the first mass-market paperbacks in Britain. The vision of Allen, John and Richard Lane, Penguin began life as an imprint of The Bodley Head, republishing existing works of fiction and non-fiction. Within a year it was a separate company, and within another few years it was commissioning new writing, launching new series and redefining the boundaries of publishing. The appearance of the classic Penguin cover design has so ingrained itself in the nation's consciousness that today, seventy years later, everybody thinks they know what a Penguin looks like. This book will show that the story of Penguin cover design is far more interesting and complicated than first impressions might suggest.

The story of the company's cover designs parallels the emergence of graphic design as a profession. This discipline, combining strategic thinking, a strong visual sense, organizational ability and the craft skills to implement them all, only developed slowly. Art schools had existed in Britain since 1858, and members of the Arts and Crafts Movement of the mid to late nineteenth century, such as William Morris and W. R. Lethaby, instigated a serious reappraisal of the role of the artist in society generally. But in the 1920s and 1930s, art for industry usually meant 'illustration' for books or 'commercial art' – poster design – for companies such as the Underground Group or Shell Petroleum, who recognized the value of artists in creating memorable publicity material. Aspects of typographic design and arrangement were studied only as part of an apprenticeship, the length and content of which was controlled by the printing industry.

Early Penguin cover design was rooted in the traditions of the print trade. But as the rebuilding of the economy after the Second World War brought about new working practices there was a merging of disciplines and changing expectations, and Penguin designs changed to reflect these developments. There started to be a separation of page design from cover design, an increasing use of commissioned designers, photographers and illustrators, and an embracing of new printing and typesetting techniques.

The developments and changes seen in Penguin covers also reflect the increasingly sophisticated attitudes of publishers and readers towards design questions. The dilemma from any publisher's point of view is whether to use a cover to promote themselves or the individual title. Part of the fascination of studying book covers is in seeing these tensions played out in practice. For Penguin, at first glance it would seem that in the 1930s the publisher's identity was the most important aspect of the design; today it would be easy to suggest that on many titles the publisher is invisible. While there are elements of truth in this – and reasons why it should be so – it fails to appreciate how many different titles and series there were in the early years (and how diverse they could be) and ignores the strong promotion of key series through consistent styling today.

This book – inevitably part history, definitely part celebration, and by design part critique – explores, through over 500 illustrations, the developments outlined above. Despite the number of covers presented, the most from a single publisher ever reproduced in one volume, it is not a catalogue: the Penguin list is just too long. It aims instead to outline the development of the brand and the introduction of new series and imprints, to show the main changes in design, and to suggest that Penguin covers are about far more than three coloured stripes and a dancing bird.

A note on book sizes

There are two standard book sizes within the paperback industry:

A format: the original Penguin size, 7 ^{1}/8 × 4 ^{3}/8 inches (181 × 111 mm).
B format: 7 ^{1}/2 × 5 inches (198 × 129 mm), first used by Penguin in 1945 for *Russian Review* and widely used over the last twenty years.

For certain series other sizes were introduced. For example, the first volumes of the Modern Painters series and Puffin Picture Books were approximately double Penguin (that is, two A-format books placed side by side). Occasionally, standard metric sizes such as A5 (210 × 148 mm) have been used, for example in the Pelican History of Art series.

A note on picture selection and reproduction of images

1. See 'Archives' in Bibliography
and Sources (p. 249).

2. *Ways of Seeing* (pp. 176–7) and
The Medium is the Massage (pp.
144–5).

Although over 500 covers may seem a lot to feature in a single book, over a
70-year period Penguin have published many thousands of titles, and many
have stayed in print for decades and had several cover designs. The final selection reflects my appreciation of that history based on research and time spent
in both of the major Penguin archives;[1] working and discussing ideas with
the book's designer and picture researcher David Pearson; and talking to past
designers and employees of the company.

While I was writing the chapter introductions David made a first selection
from the archive at Rugby. From that initial visit other titles suggested themselves, and as we each found out more, talked to past designers, and discussed
possible themes and page sequences, further titles cried out for inclusion.

I cannot claim this book to be comprehensive, because there are simply
too many stories to tell and too many books to show. The largest omission is
Puffin, whose first title is shown, but whose story is not pursued, as I felt it
was a separate story with a relationship to Penguin different from those of
other series. Also beyond the scope of this book is the mass of publicity material the company has produced to promote and describe its products. But I
have tried to explain the main strands of the history, to introduce significant
titles, series or designs, and to show, when possible, covers that have not been
reproduced in this way before.

A frustration I have with many illustrated books is the lack of a sense
of scale of the objects reproduced. This book has been designed to accommodate both of the commonly used Penguin formats at actual size. To help
make comparisons easier, reproductions have been restricted (with only two
exceptions[2]) to one of three sizes: 100 per cent, 46 per cent and 30 per cent.

In the captions, the date given is that of each book's printing as given on
its imprint page, not of the title's first publication by Penguin. Some titles retained a particular cover design for a considerable period of time, so the date
may in fact be later than the cover design. With recent publications, dates
are harder to give with any accuracy because of the practice (now common
throughout publishing) of indicating printing histories through the use of a
row of numbers (10 9 8 7 6 5 4 3 2 1) rather than giving the year of printing.

Designers, illustrators or photographers are credited as given on, or inside,
the cover. If a credit is given in [square brackets] the information is not on
the book itself and has come from other sources.

Penguin by Design

THE
PENGUINS
ARE
COMING

IF YOU WANT TO KNOW WHAT ALL THIS IS ABOUT, TURN OVER QUICKLY TO THE NEXT PAGE ⟶

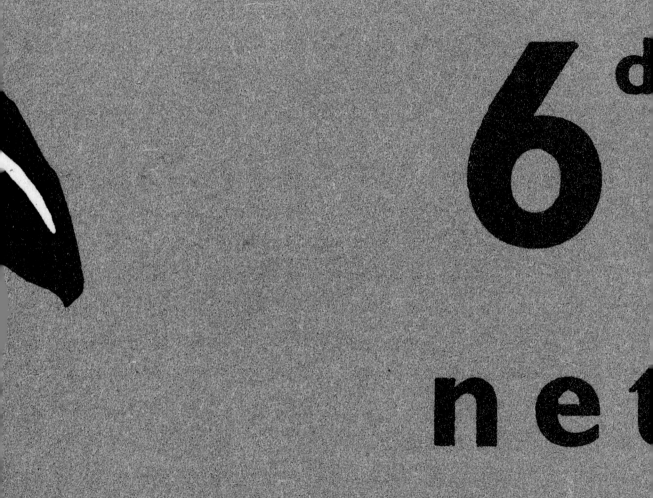

Detail taken from *Ariel*, 1935 (p. 18).

1. Establishing Paperback Publishing, 1935–46

A young Allen Lane, c. 1929

1. The Bodley Head had made its name by publishing well-designed limited edition books as well as gaining notoriety for publishing Oscar Wilde and for their journal *The Yellow Book* (1894–7). Its original art editor was Aubrey Beardsley, whose illustrations shocked polite society. By the time Allen Lane joined the firm, it had moved into more mainstream publishing and a more perilous financial state. Allen learnt the business very quickly, and soon after the firm became a public company John promoted Allen to the board. After John died in 1925, Allen inherited his position, and after John's widow died he became the majority shareholder. His younger brothers both joined the firm and became directors. Not seeing eye-to-eye with the other directors, the Lane brothers often acted as if a separate company.

2. The first ten titles were *Ariel* (André Maurois); *A Farewell to Arms* (Ernest Hemingway); *Poet's Pub* (Eric Linklater); *Madame Claire* (Susan Ertz); *The Unpleasantness at the Bellona Club* (Dorothy L. Sayers); *The Mysterious Affair at Styles* (Agatha Christie); *Twenty-five* (Beverley Nichols); *William* (E. H. Young); *Gone to Earth* (Mary Webb); and *Carnival* (Compton Mackenzie).

Penguin books were the brainchild of Allen Lane, Managing Director of The Bodley Head, a firm in which he had gained all his publishing experience under the tutelage of his relative John Lane.[1] The idea of publishing cheap, good-looking reprints of fiction and non-fiction in paperback was Allen's first and foremost, though it was refined and added to by his brothers Richard and John, also directors. Allen was inspired by the dearth of cheap reading material at Exeter train station when returning from a weekend's visit to Agatha Christie.

As the brothers soon realized, the books needed to look attractive in order to encourage shops to display them to advantage, they must be sold beyond the traditional outlets such as bookshops, and, to keep the projected price at 6d (2 $^{1}/_{2}$p: the price, often quoted, of ten cigarettes), the sales of each title must be large because the profit margin would be so small. They calculated that 17,000 copies of every title would need to be sold before any money was made.

But the board of The Bodley Head initially rejected the Lanes' proposal. The brothers then instead suggested marketing the paperbacks as though from The Bodley Head but using their own private capital, as they had done when securing the rights to the first British publication of James Joyce's *Ulysses* a year before. The board agreed and the Lanes set to work.

It seems that everyone involved in publishing at that time thought the idea was ludicrous, couldn't work and would ruin the trade. The Lanes found it difficult to obtain the rights for the ten initial titles;[2] only two came from The Bodley Head list, and Jonathan Cape's contribution of six was of crucial importance.

Having secured the list, the brothers had a dummy made of Eric Linklater's *Poet's Pub*, and then sought sales. Allen travelled the country, John took orders from his overseas contacts and Richard handled London. Orders amounted to only half the quantity needed to break even until Allen visited Woolworth's, who placed a total order for 63,500 copies and almost single-handedly saved the day.

Although 20,000 copies of each title were printed, only half of them were initially bound into covers. Such caution proved unwarranted, and the books sold immediately. The remaining printed sheets were hurriedly bound and still more copies ordered from the printers.

Paperback books did exist before the launch of Penguins on Tuesday 30

Penguin by Design

July 1935. But what their publishers all too often got wrong was the balance of price, convenience of format and excellence of scholarship, the essential elements required of cheap pocket editions ever since the printer and publisher Aldus Manutius pioneered the genre in Venice at the start of the sixteenth century. Penguin perfected the balance, combining design and sound writing to such good effect that after only ten years the name Penguin and the word 'paperback' were – much to Lane's annoyance – virtually synonymous.

With the resonance that the Penguin name rapidly acquired, it is possible to believe that the word itself was a significant element in the success. It was apparently suggested by a secretary – Joan Coles – after various alternatives had been rejected, and Edward Young, then a 21-year-old office junior, was sent to London Zoo to make sketches. He came back with the first version of the logo and the comment, 'My God, how those birds stink!'[3] The design of the books – also by Young – was simple but striking, and a reaction to the decoration or illustrative whimsy found on many other books: three horizontal stripes, the upper and lower of which were colour-coded – orange for fiction, green for crime, dark blue for biography – and a central white panel containing author and title printed black in Eric Gill's sans serif type. In the upper coloured panel was a cartouche (often referred to as a 'quartic') with the legend PENGUIN BOOKS, and in the lower panel the logo appeared. Although manufactured as paperbacks with printed covers, they came with printed dustjackets like a conventional hardback.

This 'classic' look, the one everyone knows, was not entirely new: it derived to a degree from the Albatross series of 1932. These featured simple typography designed by Hans Mardersteig, colour coding, an easily memorable bird's name and a recognizable drawing of it used as the logo.[4] Penguin books shared the same convenient format of $7^{1}/_{8} \times 4^{3}/_{8}$ inches (see p. 7), the same proportions as a Golden Section rectangle, a format favoured by printers, publishers and book designers since medieval times.

Following the extraordinary success of the launch, on 1 January 1936 Penguin Books became a separate company with a capital of £100 and with the three Lane brothers as directors. The Bodley Head name ceased to appear on the covers of the books. Later that month the milestone of one million books sold was reached, and by the time Penguin was a year old that figure had risen to 3 million. Such rapid growth dictated that new premises were required, so the company moved from the Vigo Street offices of The Bodley Head to accommodation above a car showroom in Great Portland Street, while the crypt of Holy Trinity Church on Marylebone Road served as a

Richard, Allen and John Lane outside the Penguin Head Office, 1940.

3. Quoted by Allen Lane in a speech at the opening of a Penguin exhibition at Monotype's Fetter Lane offices, 2 July 1951. Bristol Archive 16/i.

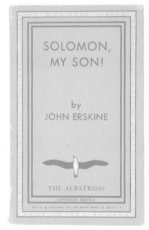

Solomon, My Son!, 1937.

4. Albatross was an English-language reprint series publishing British and American authors in countries other than the British Empire and United States. Their appearance owed much to the Tauchnitz Editions from Leipzig, initiated in 1842.

ne so insensible
ff suddenly, for
ng was wrong.

Old Style No. 2

r three weeks and
sual in conseque
s in the bundle a

Times New Roman

Lieutenant Commander E. P. Young, DSO, DSC, of HMS *Storm*. He was the first RNVR officer to command an operational submarine in the Second World War.

5. *Ten Years of Penguins: 1935–1945*, p. 12.

warehouse. This was the arrangement until a three-acre site was developed in 1937 for both offices and warehouse on the Bath Road, Harmondsworth, opposite what is now Heathrow Airport. For the next sixty years, Harmondsworth was one of the most famous addresses in publishing; as early as 1945, the little pamphlet published to mark the company's tenth anniversary could say:

It has become one of the prominent place names in bookish topography, just as the Penguin book factory has become a landmark on the Bath Road. Plain men in motor-cars, passing it, say to each other, 'That's where the Penguin Books come from,' and know that they have thereby established their stake in the cultural life of their time.[5]

In that initial period, and for some years subsequently, the basic design of the covers altered only in details. Edward Young was made the Production Manager and, as such, was responsible for typographic design. Penguin's print runs were becoming increasingly large, and several printers were used. This – and the over-long hours everyone at the firm was working – explains some of the subtle variations which occur on the cover designs. Inside, the text was originally set in Old Style No. 2, but in 1937 – during the preparation of initial designs for the Penguin Shakespeare series – a change was made to Times New Roman, which had been introduced into *The Times* (and hence proven for large runs on poor-quality paper) in 1932 and was made available to the trade in 1933. Young continued in the role of Production Manager until he joined the Royal Naval Volunteer Reserve (RNVR) in 1940, when he was succeeded by Bob Maynard and later John Overton.

The list itself changed rapidly in the first eighteen months. In addition to the reprints, Lane introduced new series to broaden the appeal of Penguin. Six Shakespeare plays appeared in April 1937, but more significant was the appearance of the first non-fiction titles under the Pelican imprint a month later (pp. 22–3). In 1936 Lane had asked George Bernard Shaw to let him publish *The Intelligent Woman's Guide to Socialism, Capitalism and Sovietism*. Shaw responded positively and offered to write a new section explaining Bolshevism and Fascism. This was the first original writing published by the company, and Lane found other 'intellectual' titles to sit alongside it and create a non-fiction series. He appointed V. K. Krishna Menon as Editor, with Peter Chalmers-Mitchell, H. L. Beales and W. E. Williams as advisors. As it developed, the list embraced writing on politics, economics, social sciences, literature and the visual arts, and from the start there was no rigorous dividing line between Pelican and Penguin subject areas. The design of Pelicans followed the horizontal stripes of the Penguins but with a pale blue colour and a pelican logo drawn, like the penguin, by Edward Young.

The development of Penguin in the few years before the outbreak of war was very much dependent on the personalities of the Lane brothers and those they grew to trust. Of the Pelican advisors, Williams soon became the key figure, and a secretary newly appointed in 1937, Eunice Frost, was before long recognized as a superb editor and became the lynchpin of everything that happened at Harmondsworth until her retirement in 1960.

In November 1937 the publishing programme was further broadened with the launch of Penguin's first periodical (pp. 36–7), *Penguin Parade*, and the publication of the first Penguin Special, Edgar Mowrer's *Germany Puts the Clock Back* (pp. 28–31). *Penguin Parade* was followed by several more periodicals,[6] but it was the Specials that made Penguin's expansion and its domination of the paperback market possible. These were topical publications that, in the eighteen months between their initiation and the outbreak of war, dealt mainly with the rapidly developing political issues of the time. The urgency of the subject matter was reflected in the speed of production (four weeks from typescript to bookshop) and in their cover designs. The Specials featured headlines on the covers, many stripes, and different variants of the Gill Sans typeface used with almost Victorian abandon. The political Specials sold 100,000 copies in a matter of weeks, compared to typical fiction sales of around 40,000 in three or four months. Thus the series contributed hugely to the company's cashflow, and the sales figures in the pre-war years would dictate what Penguin could achieve during the war itself.

Further new series appeared before the war: the short-lived Illustrated Classics were launched in May 1938 (pre-dating Penguin Classics proper by eight years; pp. 24–5), the county-by-county Penguin Guides in March 1939, and the hardbacked and illustrated King Penguins in November 1939 (pp. 26–7 and 76–7). The Kings were initially edited by Elizabeth Senior, but her role was taken over by Nikolaus Pevsner – author of *Pioneers of Modern Design* (1936) – after her death in an air raid in 1941. It marked the beginning of a long and fruitful relationship between Penguin and Pevsner, and was one of several prominent associations between the company and respected academics.

War was eventually declared on 3 September 1939, and Penguin, while also benefiting from happy accidents – such as the discovery that a battledress pocket could accommodate a Penguin as if made for it – was better placed

William Emrys Williams

Eunice Frost

6. *Penguin Hansard*, August 1940; *New Writing*, November 1940; *Transatlantic*, September 1943; *New Biology*, July 1945; *Russian Review*, October 1945; *Science News*, June 1946; *Film Review*, August 1946; and *Music Magazine*, February 1947.

Nikolaus Pevsner

7. John Lane was killed in action
when his ship, HMS *Avenger*, was
sunk on 15 November 1942.

Noel Carrington

Eleanor Graham

than most other publishers to deal with wartime conditions. When paper rationing was introduced in 1940, allocations were calculated as a percentage of paper consumption in the twelve months before hostilities began. Penguin, although handicapped by the restrictions, had a far greater allocation than most other publishers. The typographic standards that were introduced at the same time, specifying among other things the ratio of text area to page size, could be easily met. And the key to everything was the personality of Allen Lane – who remained at Harmondsworth to run the firm after John and Richard joined the RNVR and were called up[7] – ready to seize every opportunity to use Penguin Books as a positive force in the war effort while not forgetting the good of the company. In this, it was a great advantage that one of his most influential editors, W. E. Williams, had a leading role in the Army Bureau of Current Affairs (ABCA), which backed many initiatives that enabled Penguins to be distributed in large quantities to British and Allied soldiers across the globe. Thousands of Penguins formed a large proportion of the books sent via the Services Central Book Club (SCBC) from 1940; in 1942 a Forces Book Club was set up to print editions of books to be distributed through the army's own channels; and an EVT (educational and vocational training) and 'release' scheme was established in 1941, a Prisoner of War book scheme in 1943, and Services Editions in 1945.

As if that wasn't enough, new series were also being launched for the population at large, who were now without many other sources of entertainment. Penguin Poets first appeared in June 1941, Planning, Design and Art books in April 1942, Handbooks in December and Reference in April 1943.

As thousands of city children faced wartime evacuation, Lane launched Puffin Picture Books in December 1940 (following up a pre-war suggestion by Noel Carrington, who then edited the series until the early 1960s; pp. 34–5), and a year later Puffin Story Books appeared, under the guidance of Eleanor Graham. The picture books were noteworthy for their use of colour printing from auto-lithography (in which the artist draws directly on to the printing plate) and their larger format – approximately twice as wide but the same height as a normal Penguin – while the standard-sized story books featured illustrations from the outset.

A desire to give the public access to art at a time when the principal London galleries had evacuated their collections to safer places resulted in the Modern Painters series (pp. 42–3). The first four titles, Henry Moore, Graham Sutherland, Duncan Grant and Paul Nash, appeared in April 1944. Similar in size to Puffin Picture Books, they contained twelve pages of text and thirty-two pages of plates, sixteen in colour. While the series editor was Sir Kenneth Clark, Director of the National Gallery, credit for much of the organization and realization of the series lay with Eunice Frost. Somehow, good paper was obtained, paintings were tracked down for photography, and high standards of colour reproduction were achieved under incredibly difficult circumstances.

In 1945, between VE Day and the dropping of the first atomic bomb, Penguin celebrated its tenth birthday with, among other events, the publication of *Ten Years of Penguins: 1935–1945* as a tribute to what had been achieved during that time. It was simply a piece of publicity, up-beat, confident, self-congratulatory – and rightly so. It was not its role to analyse the future of paperback publishing and how competition would affect Penguin. Alongside celebrating its tenth anniversary, Penguin, with its leftish political leanings, was seen by some to have had a role in the Labour Party's euphoric post-war election victory, and, in another indication of their apparently inexorable growth, in January 1946 a further new series appeared, the Penguin Classics, the first title being E. V. Rieu's translation of Homer's *Odyssey*. As a new generation of people grew up with Penguin as a central part of the country's cultural life, its future seemed assured.

Emile Victor Rieu

Ariel, 1935.
[The accent in the author's name
only appears from the second
cover printing on.]

The horizontal grid, 1935

The first Penguin titles appeared at a time when the various roles of designer, art director and printer were not clearly differentiated. The basic horizontal tripartite division of the covers, as well as the penguin itself, were devised by Edward Young, who became the company's first Production Manager. The colours used to indicate subject matter – initially just orange for fiction, green for crime, dark blue for biography, cerise for travel & adventure, red for plays – were an aspect of the design which far outlasted the original layout.

The design featured typefaces popular at that time. Bodoni Ultra Bold – a *faux* nineteenth-century revival – was used within the quartic for the publisher's name, while two weights of the relatively new (1927–8) Gill Sans were used for the remainder of the front cover and spine information. Although the imprint was PENGUIN BOOKS the publisher was THE BODLEY HEAD, whose name remained on the front for eighty titles until Penguin became a separate company. The price was printed not on the cover itself but on the dustjacket, which in all other respects was identical to the cover it protected.

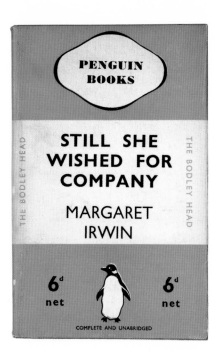

Still She Wished for Company (dustjacket), 1937.

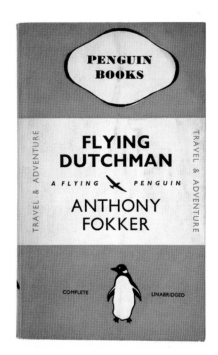

Flying Dutchman, 1938.

The horizontal grid: variations

The Gun, 1939.

The original cover design had a tremendous impact in bookshops, appearing very fresh and modern with its directness. It was an important element in attracting new customers to book-buying and in inspiring confidence in the new publisher.

Despite the apparent unity of appearance, during the quarter-century of their use there were as many as twelve main front cover variations and eleven kinds of back cover.

Illustrations appeared on a few titles, almost apologetically in the case of *Flying Dutchman* (p. 19), and more positively on *The Gun*. The only cover in which illustration is both positively used and successfully integrated into the design is *The Compleat Angler*. The wood engraving is by Gertrude Hermes, who also worked on Richard Jefferies' *The Story of My Heart* in the Illustrated Classics series of 1938.

The Compleat Angler, 1939.
[Wood engraving by
Gertrude Hermes.]

The Penguin logo was redrawn several times in the first twelve years. Versions included the lifelike but awkward original (pp. 18–19), a dancing penguin (*A Room of One's Own*), and the 1939 version (*The Gun*), which is very close to that used today.

The number of titles and the size of their print runs meant that several printers were needed to produce the books. Even before wartime economies and labour shortages, staff were overworked and quality control of some of the typographic details was lacking. Several titles – including *Lawrence of Arabia* – use other variations of the Gill Sans type family; *Siamese White* uses the alternative capital 'W' in its title.

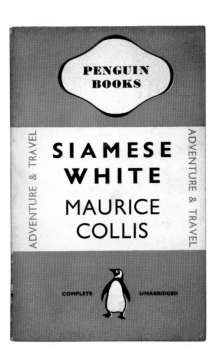

Lawrence of Arabia/Zionism and Palestine, 1940.

Siamese White, 1940.

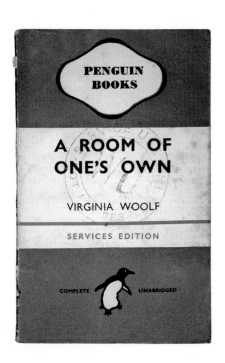

A Room of One's Own, 1945.

Murder by Burial, 1943.

Original writing:
the first Pelicans, 1937

The Intelligent Woman's Guide to Socialism, Capitalism, Sovietism & Fascism, 1937.

The first Pelican Books appeared in May 1937 and included two volumes of George Bernard Shaw's *The Intelligent Woman's Guide to Socialism, Capitalism, Sovietism & Fascism*. Shaw wrote two new chapters for the Pelican edition, and this was the first time that a piece of previously unpublished writing had appeared in a Penguin imprint.

The series was intended to present serious subjects to the 'interested layman' and was an immediate success, which surprised even Allen Lane, who wrote a year later:

Who would have imagined that, even at 6d, there was a thirsty public anxious to buy thousands of copies of books on science, sociology, economics, archaeology, astronomy, and other equally serious subjects.

(Edwards and Hare, p. 13)

Reading for Profit, 1945.

Edward Young drew two new logos for Pelican (a flying pelican for the cover, and one standing for the spine) and for the cover layout used the horizontal grid of the general list but with blue as the Pelican colour. The imprint PELICAN BOOKS was set within the quartic and in Gill Sans from the start. As with *The Compleat Angler* (p. 20), the cover layout could be altered to accommodate a simple line illustration.

Some Pelicans also appeared as 'Pelican Specials', and their design mimicked the standard Special design (*Modern German Art*, *Blue Angels and Whales*, *Microbes by the Million* and *Hydroponics*).

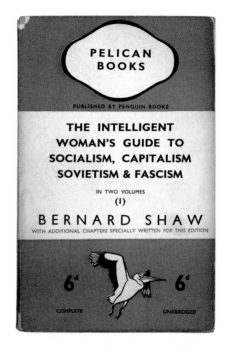

Penguin by Design

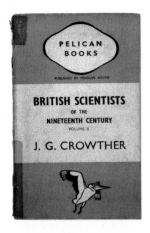

British Scientists of the Nineteenth Century, Volume 2, 1941.

Metals in the Service of Man, 1944.

Explosives, 1942.

An Introduction to Modern Architecture, 1941.

Film, 1944.
[The cover shows a still from Sergei Eisenstein's film Battleship Potemkin, 1925.]

Modern German Art, 1938.

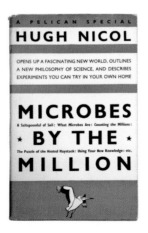

Blue Angels and Whales, 1938.
[Cover illustration by Robert Gibbings.]

Microbes by the Million, 1939.

Hydroponics, 1940.

Penguin Illustrated Classics, 1938

Walden, 1938. [Wood engravings by Ethelbert White.]

The idea behind the Illustrated Classics was as straightforward as that behind Penguin itself: to make available to everybody something which had previously been the preserve of those with money. The first ten books were titles that were out of copyright; the money saved on royalties could be put instead towards commissioning the illustrators.

Lane chose as series Art Editor the artist Robert Gibbings, the owner of the Golden Cockerell Press from 1924 to 1933 and an important patron of wood engravers. Wood engraving had been used for book illustration since printing was invented and was undergoing something of a revival in the 1930s, with many of its leading practitioners emerging from London's influential Central School of Arts & Crafts.

Typee, 1938. [Wood engravings by Robert Gibbings.]

The covers for these books were re-designed with a vertical emphasis and a large central white area to accommodate an illustration. The weight and feel of the illustration was matched by the use of Albertus (designed by Berthold Wolpe in 1932) for the author's name and the title. In addition to the cover, there was an illustrated title page – each complete with its own unique penguin – and smaller illustrations throughout the text. The series was not considered a financial success and no further titles were issued.

Penguin by Design

WALDEN
or, Life in the Woods
by
HENRY DAVID THOREAU

PENGUIN BOOKS LIMITED
HARMONDSWORTH MIDDLESEX ENGLAND

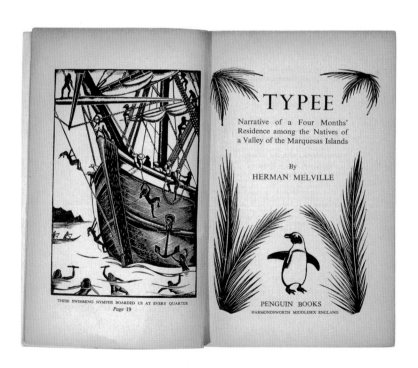

THESE SWIMMING NYMPHS BOARDED US AT EVERY QUARTER
Page 19

TYPEE

Narrative of a Four Months'
Residence among the Natives of
a Valley of the Marquesas Islands

By
HERMAN MELVILLE

PENGUIN BOOKS
HARMONDSWORTH MIDDLESEX ENGLAND

King Penguins, 1939

Penguin's first venture into hardback publishing was a disparate series of books designed on quite different principles from the rest of the Penguin list. The Kings were conceived as a series of beautifully designed collectable books, imitating the Insel-Bücherei series that had been published in Leipzig since 1912.

The first titles appeared in November 1939: *British Birds on Lake, River and Stream* and *A Book of Roses*, each based around much earlier books and on subjects likely to attract the public's attention and sell well. Priced at one shilling, the break-even point for these titles was 20,000 copies. Considerable care went into their production, which used colour printing on a scale not seen before in Britain for this kind of book. In 1941 R. B. Fishenden was employed as technical supervisor, and despite the many wartime restrictions quality was maintained.

Although some titles relied on a formulaic design of patterned background with typography set within a bordered panel, there was considerable variety and free use was made of whatever style of illustration or design suited each book's subject matter. This only increased their attractiveness and appeal.

The series continued until 1959, and its further development is described on pages 76–7.

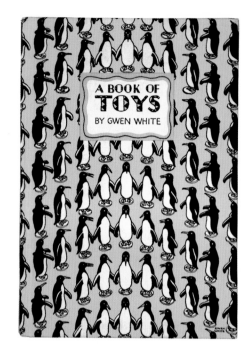

The Bayeux Tapestry, 1949.
Cover design by William Grimmond.

OPPOSITE: *Popular English Art*, 1945. Cover design by Clarke Hutton.

Ourselves and Germany
(dustjacket), 1938.

The Marquess of Londonderry

OURSELVES AND GERMANY

SHOULD BRITAIN REGARD GERMANY AS HER POTENTIAL ENEMY, OR SEEK HER FRIEND-SHIP? LORD LONDONDERRY THINKS WE SHOULD ADOPT A POLICY OF FRIENDSHIP WITH HITLER AND A BETTER UNDER-STANDING OF GERMANY'S AIMS

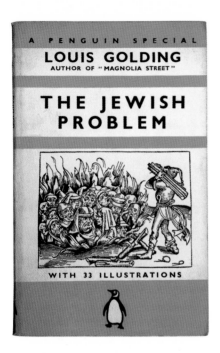

A sense of urgency:
Penguin Specials, 1937

Fulfilling a purpose not unlike the investigative journalism and current affairs television programmes of today, Penguin Specials first appeared in November 1937.

The subjects for Specials had to be of immediate and pressing concern and, once identified, authoritative writers were commissioned to write to almost impossible deadlines. While there were one or two anomalies in the list, the titles commissioned before and during the war tell the story of a country trying to come to terms with world events and with its role and responsibilities.

In terms of design, the tripartite division and use of orange gave way to a more aggressively striped layout. Typographic restraint was abandoned, with extensive 'blurb' appearing on some designs and a layout which has much in common with Victorian handbills.

Some continuity with the rest of the Penguin list was maintained by using the bolder weights of the Gill Sans typeface on many titles. Of the other faces used, Rockwell Shadow (*Our Food Problem*, p. 30) seems to have been the favourite second choice, followed by Bodoni Ultra Bold (*New Ways of War*, p. 31). In addition to typeface variants, other printer's devices – such as rules, stars and fists – were used to enliven the covers. Illustration and photography were also occasionally used.

Towards the end of the war the cover design, reflecting the changed nature of the titles themselves, became simpler, almost reverting to the proportions of the original tripartite grid.

The Jewish Problem, 1938.

One Man against Europe, 1939.

I Was Hitler's Prisoner, 1939.

Between 2 Wars? (dustjacket),
1939.

Germany – What Next?, 1939.

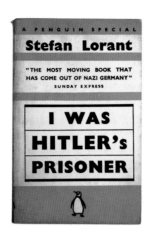

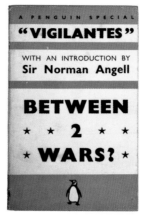

China Struggles for Unity
(dustjacket), 1939.

The New German Empire
(dustjacket), 1939.

Why Britain is at War (dustjacket), 1939.

Our Food Problem, 1939.

The Penguin Political Atlas, 1940.

The Rights of Man, 1940.

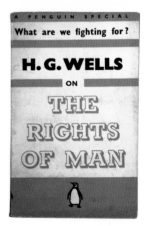

Penguin by Design

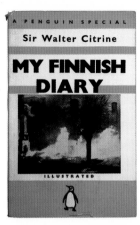

Unser Kampf: Our Struggle
(dustjacket), 1940.

My Finnish Diary (dustjacket),
1940.

The Common Sense of War and
Peace, 1940.

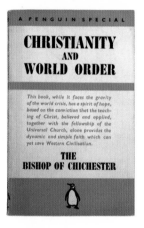

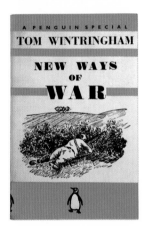

Christianity and World Order,
1940.

New Ways of War, 1940.

Aircraft Recognition, 1941.

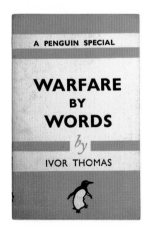

Warfare by Words, 1942.

Our Settlement with Germany,
1944.

Lend-Lease, 1944.

Subsidising production:
selling advertising space, 1938

While Rome Burns, 1940.

Early Penguin books carried listings of other available titles on the back covers and on any blank pages at the back of the book itself. Sometimes particular titles were promoted in the form of an advertisement (below). In February 1938 the first commercial advertisements appeared, and the revenue they generated helped keep the cover price at the original sixpence for a time. The use of adverts declined rapidly from about 1944.

Christianity and World Order, 1940.

Sporting Adventure, 1943.

Penguin by Design

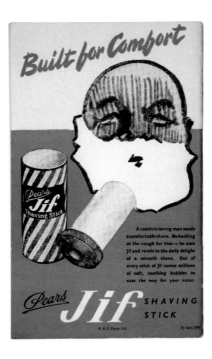

I. Establishing Paperback Publishing, 1935–46

For children:
Puffin Picture Books, 1940

OPPOSITE: *War on Land*, 1940. [Cover illustration by James Holland.]

Many of the early series came about because Allen Lane had a hunch that a particular idea would work, and often to those around him it seemed no more than blind optimism. In most cases he knew enough about a subject to be sure of his own judgement, and he knew who to employ to make the idea work. But children's books were different.

Noel Carrington, an authority on printing and design, had first suggested the idea of a series of illustrated children's books to Lane before the war. Carrington had already worked out that if they were printed by lithography rather than letterpress, thirty-two-page books could be printed with sixteen in colour and sixteen in black and the price could still be kept at sixpence. Lane did not pursue the matter immediately, but once war broke out and children were being evacuated from the cities he proceeded with haste, and Puffin Picture Books were launched in December 1940. Three of the first four concerned the war, on land, on sea and in the air, while the fourth was *On the Farm*.

The artists involved worked at the printers, drawing directly on to the stone (printing surface), which was unusual for the period and would have been vetoed by the print unions if it had been peacetime.

Artistically they were well received, but they were not universally liked by booksellers because of their awkward, flimsy format. Despite this, they established a market for well-produced children's literature, and a year later the first Puffin Story Books emerged under the editorship of Eleanor Graham.

A PUFFIN
PICTURE BOOK

No. 1

War on Land

by James Holland

Periodicals

New Biology, Volume 1, 1946.

A major factor in Penguin's early success was Allen Lane's keen sense of timing and his eye for opportunity. During the war there was a greater need for reading matter of all kinds because so many forms of entertainment were curtailed or non-existent. Several periodicals were started and allowed to continue as long as they made money.

In design terms they are mixed in appearance; the only titles that have any visual link to the main series are *Penguin Parade* and *Hansard*.

Russian Review is notable for being the first Penguin publication to use the larger B format, while the 1947 *Science News* looked forward to the sobriety that was to come.

OPPOSITE: *Science News*, Volume 1, 1946.

Russian Review, Volume 1, 1945.

The Penguin New Writing, Volume 1, 1941.

The Penguin Hansard, Volume 1, 1940.

OPPOSITE: *Penguin Parade*, Volume 1, 1937.

The Penguin Film Review, Volume 1, 1946.

Penguin by Design

SCIENCE
NEWS

I

ONE
SHILLING

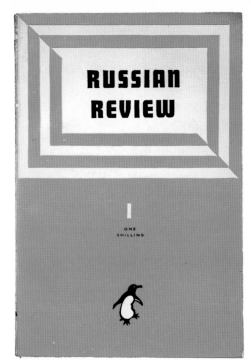

RUSSIAN
REVIEW

I

ONE
SHILLING

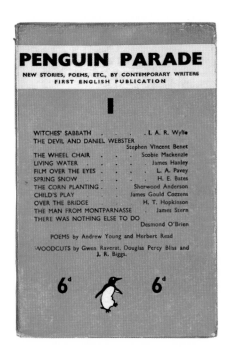

PENGUIN PARADE
NEW STORIES, POEMS, ETC., BY CONTEMPORARY WRITERS
FIRST ENGLISH PUBLICATION

I

WITCHES' SABBATH . . . . . I. A. R. Wylie
THE DEVIL AND DANIEL WEBSTER
Stephen Vincent Benet
THE WHEEL CHAIR . . . . Scobie Mackenzie
LIVING WATER . . . . . . James Hanley
FILM OVER THE EYES . . . . . L. A. Pavey
SPRING SNOW . . . . H. E. Bates
THE CORN PLANTING . . . Sherwood Anderson
CHILD'S PLAY . . . . James Gould Cozzens
OVER THE BRIDGE . . . . H. T. Hopkinson
THE MAN FROM MONTPARNASSE . . James Stern
THERE WAS NOTHING ELSE TO DO
Desmond O'Brien

POEMS by Andrew Young and Herbert Read

WOODCUTS by Gwen Raverat, Douglas Percy Bliss and
J. R. Biggs.

6ᵈ   6ᵈ

The Penguin
FILM REVIEW

CONTENTS
I

Anthony Asquith
THE TENTH MUSE CLIMBS PARNASSUS

Michael Balcon
BRITISH FEATURE FILMS DURING THE WAR

Michael Powell
MANVELL GRILLS POWELL

Richard Winnington
A CRITIQUE OF CONTEMPORARY CINEMA

Catherine de la Roche
RECENT DEVELOPMENTS IN SOVIET CINEMA

one shilling

Transatlantic, September 1943.

Transatlantic, October 1943.
Cover illustration by Wilfred Fryer.

A special relationship: *Transatlantic*, 1943

The editor of *Transatlantic*, Geoffrey Crowther, stated in the introduction to the first issue that it was to be 'a monthly commentary, from the British point of view, of what is going on in America'. This appeared in September 1943 after the first Allied landings in mainland Europe had been made secure and the course of the war seemed more certain. Among the members of the Editorial Committee was Alistair Cooke, later to gain fame as the long-running presenter of 'Letter from America' on the BBC's Home Service (later renamed Radio 4).

The covers depict aspects of the two countries' war efforts or the close ties which linked them. The illustrations, like those on Puffin Picture Books, were printed lithographically.

Transatlantic, January 1944.
Cover illustration by Xenia.

Transatlantic, April 1944.
Cover illustration by Eric Fraser.

Serenade, 1947. [Cover illustration by Robert Jonas.]

The Unbearable Bassington, 1947. [Cover illustration by Robert Jonas.]

 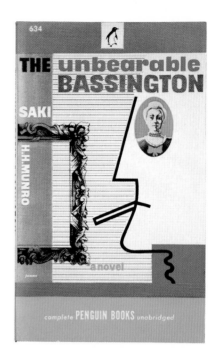

The Odyssey, 1947. [Cover illustration by Robert Jonas.]

The Velvet Well, 1947. [Cover illustration by Robert Jonas.]

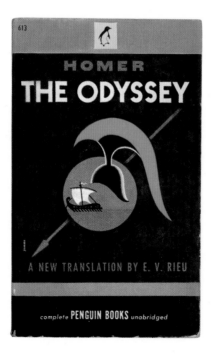 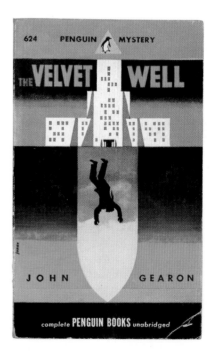

Penguin by Design

A short-lived freedom: American Penguin covers, 1942–7

The first overseas Penguin office was established in New York in 1938. Set up by John Lane and run by Kurt Enoch and Ian Ballantine, its purpose was to act as an import agent for books printed in Britain. The importation of books stopped after the attack on Pearl Harbor (December 1941), and Penguin Books Inc. started to produce its own titles. It marketed them in a way that suited America, where books were often sold alongside magazines and had, therefore, to compete directly with them.

After John Lane's death in 1942, various administrative problems ensued. They were compounded by differences of opinion between Allen Lane and Ian Ballantine, who then left the firm in 1945 to found Bantam Books and was replaced by Victor Weybright. For new titles in the list, Weybright commissioned many illustrations from the artist Robert Jonas. These distinctive covers, which owe much to the kinds of commercial art then appearing in advertising, are a world away from the covers of British Penguins, which still relied on the typographic traditions of the printing trades.

Despite the emphasis on illustration there is a strong sense of branding at work here, with clear zones at top and bottom for the logo and the imprint. The Penguin logo used is slightly different from the contemporary British versions, while the Pelican has been elegantly restyled.

Public Opinion, 1946. [Cover illustration by Robert Jonas.]

The Birth and Death of the Sun, 1945. [Cover illustration by Robert Jonas.]

Penguin Modern Painters, 1944

Conceived as a way of bringing art to people at a time when the national collections had been packed off to safe locations in the countryside, Modern Painters was benevolent propaganda that also helped to establish the careers of several young British artists.

A series of this sort had been suggested by Kenneth Clark, Director of the National Gallery, to W. E. Williams, who then presented it to Allen Lane. Once the idea was agreed, Clark took care of the art, the selection of artists – many of them his friends – and the commissioning of the essay writers. Eunice Frost took care of all the organization, from finding the paintings to be photographed to writing captions and checking dates.

The most significant aspect of the books was the colour reproduction, which was overseen by R. B. Fishenden, Editor of *The Penrose Annual*. Great care was taken, firstly with the photography, then with the block-making and proofing, to ensure that the colour was as accurate as possible. Because the books were considered propaganda, Lane had managed to secure an allocation of art paper to print on, which meant that the finished product did not look as though it had been produced during wartime. The first titles appeared in April 1944 and a further two followed before the end of the war.

Their covers are all very straightforward and in three main styles. Most versions also had a dustjacket with a full-colour image.

Edward Burra, 1945.

Ben Shahn, 1947.

RALPH TUBB

LIVING IN CI

LONG AGO

YESTERDAY

TO-DAY

Post-war reconstruction

Just as the pre-war Specials discussed the difficulties of that period, Penguins published during and immediately after the war often aimed to explain aspects of recovery. Many of these books focused on architecture and planning and followed Puffin Picture Books in using a double-A format. There was no overall series look to the covers, with some titles having a hint of the pre-war amateurishness about them while others show a much greater awareness of contemporary design developments. *Living in Cities* falls into the latter category, using photographs in a cinematic sequence to reinforce the arguments contained within and to reflect the initial optimism for the large-scale rebuilding that would be necessary in the post-war period.

Living in Cities, 1942.

The first Classic, 1946

The publication of the Classics is another example of Allen Lane allowing his intuition to prevail over the contrary advice of others.

Several versions of *The Odyssey* were in print when E. V. Rieu offered his own translation to Penguin for consideration. Rieu, born in 1887, had previously been Educational Manager at Methuen and had edited *A Book of Latin Poetry* for them in 1925. This translation of *The Odyssey* originated in Rieu's habit of translating aloud for his wife, who encouraged him to write it down. Lane read two chapters and was convinced, and upon publication it was an immediate success, becoming Penguin's best-selling title until *Lady Chatterley's Lover* in 1960. It was also the first of a series which Rieu himself edited until 1964 and which of course continues today.

The design was by John Overton, who was then Production Manager. The typeface is Eric Gill's Perpetua, designed in 1928. Although the layout was rather clumsy, its classicism reflected the subject matter and featured a circular illustration – known as a roundel – by William Grimmond. Rieu was unhappy with this as it shows a boat under full sail but with oars in use. The roundel was redrawn for the 1959 reprinting (see no. 6 on p. 66), but this mistake was not corrected.

Colours for the series seem to have been thought about from the start (p. 64), and brown indicated Greek titles. Only the first seven titles appeared in this design, before it was restyled by Jan Tschichold in 1947–8.

The Odyssey roundel artwork by William Grimmond, *c.*1945.

HOMER

THE

ODYSSEY

A NEW TRANSLATION BY

E. V. RIEU

E. V. Rieu

Allen Lane

J. E. Morpurgo

R. B. Fishenden

W. E. Williams

Richard Lane

Noel Carrington

II. Consistency and Competition, 1947–59

Eunice Frost

A. W. Haslett

Alan Glover

C. A. Mace

Michael Abercrombie

Nikolaus Pevsner

A. J. Ayer

Gordon Jacob

M. L. Johnson

Eleanor Graham

Max Mallowan

John Lehmann

Detail taken from *After the Conference: The Penguin Editors*, 1955, by Rodrigo Moynihan (oil on canvas, 10 × 14 feet).

II. Consistency and Competition, 1947–59

1. In Lamb, p. 40.

Jan Tschichold

2. Bristol Archive, DM1294 16/1.

When Beatrice Warde, one of Britain's leading typographic evangelists, said, 'The typographic planning of the early Penguins was an exercise in discipline, good manners and economic realism which would have reflected credit on the most mature designer,'[1] she was being a little generous. Before the war, the inside of a Penguin book – although improved after the introduction of Times New Roman in 1937 – was pleasant only in an ordinary way. There was a straightforwardness to the pages, which Lane liked, but nothing to lift them above that. In addition, the handling of headings, titles and other display matter was not of a uniform standard, being very much at the whim of individual printers.

After the war, those same problems remained but were compounded by ongoing shortages of both staff and materials at many printers. Lane recognized that he needed to raise the standard of his books, not only because it had fallen so low, but also as a way of responding to the inevitable emergence of new paperback publishers. Lane had wanted Oliver Simon of Curwen Press – author of *Introduction to Typography* (Faber & Faber, 1945) and a leading exponent of the 'reformed traditional' style – to work for him, but Simon was unavailable. He recommended instead the most famous typographer of the day, Jan Tschichold. A visit by Lane and Simon to Switzerland confirmed the wisdom of the idea, and in March 1947 Tschichold took over in charge of typography and production at Harmondsworth for a salary higher than that of any other employee.

Jan Tschichold was born in 1902 and became apprenticed to a printer. He gained early fame through his writing, first *Elementare Typographie* in 1925 and then *Die neue Typographie* in 1928. These works played a crucial role in the popularization of the 'new typography': asymmetric, sans serif and modern. In 1933 he was dismissed from his teaching post in Munich by the National Socialists and emigrated to Switzerland, where in 1935 he published *Typographische Gestaltung* (*Asymmetric Typography*, 1967). He moved away from the new typography, which he began to associate with fascism, shortly before the war and began to work in a reformed classical manner using serif typefaces and centred arrangements. It was this later work which Oliver Simon admired and which Allen Lane wanted to apply to Penguins.

Described later by Lane as 'a mild man with an inflexible character',[2] Tschichold had asked for examples of books in advance of his taking up the post, and sent annotated criticisms ahead of his arrival. He looked at every aspect of Penguin typography: the text setting within the books, the Penguin logo, and the book covers themselves.

During his time at the company (1947–9) he re-educated all its printers about standards and consistency in typesetting. These were famously brought together as the *Penguin Composition Rules*, originally a four-page leaflet containing concise and precise instructions on typographic style. Among his most influential instructions was 'Capitals must be letterspaced'.[3] The Penguin logo had undergone several changes in twelve years of use, and Tschichold redrew Edward Young's 1939 version to create a definitive model. It lasted until 2003.

The standard and distinctive tripartite cover was given a facelift. Three small changes – a more consistent use of the Gill Sans typeface with slight letterspacing, a thin rule between title and author, and a consistent use of space – made for a far more distinguished cover. Not all of these changes appeared immediately, and Tschichold had to spend much time setting out clear written instructions for these and all other aspects of his reforms.

Other series' cover designs were also improved: the attempted classicism of the Classics design of 1946 was properly realized from no. 8 onwards, and similar bordered designs were introduced for the Shakespeare and poetry titles as well as the Pelican series. These covers and the many title pages Tschichold designed are where his absolute mastery of spatial arrangement shows through most clearly. But Tschichold's time at Penguin was cut short by a worsening exchange rate, and he returned to Switzerland in 1949, having recommended Hans Schmoller, an employee of Curwen Press, as his successor.

Like Tschichold, Hans Schmoller was born and grew up in Germany and was apprenticed to a printer. As a Jew in the 1930s he faced increasing restrictions under the Nazi's anti-Semitic regime, but he was able to visit Britain in 1937 and then secured a job in South Africa in 1938, where he remained for the duration of the war. At the Morija Printing Works (in today's Lesotho) he worked in the same 'reformed traditionalism' as Oliver Simon and began a correspondence with him. Schmoller became a British citizen in 1946 and the following year came to Britain to work, joining the Curwen Press for a short time before moving to Penguin after receiving Tschichold's endorsement.

It was chiefly as a text designer that Schmoller made his mark. On Penguin's twenty-first birthday, *Printing Review* summed up Schmoller's achievement:

[He] substantially took over the main features of Tschichold's style and then brought it to a close perfection by additional subtleties and refinements. The dryness and severity of the present Penguin manner is widely admired,

3. Previously, the letters were set without any spacing adjustments, and awkward letter combinations such as AW in the middle of a word would leave a visual 'hole'.

Hans Schmoller

4. Burbidge and Gray, p. 18.

5. David Bann, in Cinamon, pp. 39–40.

especially by those who understand the depth of skill and taste which go to achieve it.[4]

It was a design based on sound principles and well-tried practices, although Schmoller, like Tschichold before him, had to repeat the same insistent instructions about 'optically even letterspacing' time after time. Schmoller gained a reputation for his fastidiousness and ability to notice minute variation of detail. He earned the nickname Half-Point Schmoller, 'The only man who could distinguish between a Bembo full point and a Garamond full point at 200 paces'.[5]

By the early 1950s the texts of Penguin books were of a typographical standard achieved by no other British paperback publisher; but the covers seemed sadly out of time. Although the horizontal tripartite covers are now regarded affectionately as classics of style, they did not address the increasing competition from other publishers nor the simple fact that, with over 700 titles in print, greater visual differentiation might be a good thing.

Schmoller worked up an idea begun by Tschichold and his assistant Erik Ellegaard Frederiksen: a vertical grid (pp. 78–84). In this design, the central white area was flanked by narrower colour-coded bands and had room for the title, the author's name and either some selling copy ('blurb') or an illustration. The resulting covers – which first appeared in 1951 – elegantly balanced the need for some form of attractive visual differentiation with the desire to retain a strongly branded overall image.

But still the style and feel of the early versions is decidedly old-fashioned, with black or two-colour line drawings of a kind more typical of pre-war days or the black and white pages of magazines such as the *Radio Times*. It was evident that further refinements were required, and other subtle changes were introduced on these covers: the typeface Corvinus was used for titles by Aldous Huxley, for example, and certain authors received their own monograms as additional identifiers. The use of illustrations was further increased, with Schmoller commissioning new talent in the shape of graduates from the Royal College of Art such as David Gentleman. Despite this, the vertical grid imposed significant constraints, and there is clearly a hesitancy about whether to respect or infringe the orange borders: however well-intentioned, many covers simply appear awkward.

Penguin's editorial range continued to spread during this period. In 1951 *Cornwall* and *Nottinghamshire* appeared as the first two of Nikolaus Pevsner's magnificent Buildings of England series (pp. 72–3). Originally paperback, they appeared with a cover design similar to the Classics, complete with a circular line drawing. Their text pages are notable for the clarity Schmoller achieved by using only one weight and size of the typeface Plantin. The series took Pevsner until 1974 to complete, and even the most recently updated volumes (now published by Yale University Press) still follow the essence of Schmoller's scheme. Pevsner was also editor of the Pelican History of Art, the first two volumes of which appeared in 1953. Originally proposed in 1946, this was Penguin's first venture into large-format, mainstream hardback publishing and was a surprising success.

In 1954 a different kind of milestone was reached with the publication of no. 1000 in the general Penguin list.[6] Given Allen Lane's unease at publishing books about the war – which allowed other publishers to develop that market almost exclusively – his gesture of publishing Edward Young's *One of Our Submarines* as no. 1000 was all the more remarkable.

Throughout the 1950s competition was growing. Publishers such as Pan (founded in 1944 by Alan Bott with backing from Collins, Macmillan and Hodder & Stoughton) and Corgi (1951) had a more targeted readership and quite different approaches to marketing their titles, and they didn't seem to pose an immediate threat to Penguin, whose comprehensive list covered most aspects of human knowledge and recreation. Despite apparent complacency, however, Penguin began to realize that the vertical grid, with its ill-fitting and often old-fashioned illustrations, was perhaps too reticent in the face of a competition using full-colour imagery and dynamic lettering on their titles. But Schmoller was not the kind of designer to produce that sort of active cover, nor to devise a structure to contain the kind of illustration that might compete in an overcrowded market.

When John Curtis (1928–2005), who joined as assistant to Eunice Frost in 1952 and then became Publicity Manager, returned from a six-month visit to the USA in 1956 he took a much more active role in the design of covers. Photography and full-bleed images were being increasingly used (pp. 92–3) and a decision was taken at Board level to conduct a far more controlled experiment involving four-colour illustrated covers. Schmoller offered Abram Games the job of Art Director for the new series.

Abram Games (1914–96) was best known for his poster work for the Ministry of Propaganda during the war and also for designing the emblem for the Festival of Britain in 1951. At the initial briefing, Games was shown designs by Robert Jonas and others produced in Penguin's New York offices during the war (pp. 40–41). Making good use of coloured panels and a kind

6. Each Penguin series was numbered sequentially from the start. When new series were introduced they were given a series prefix, for example A for Pelicans, and therefore their own number sequence.

John Curtis

of painterly collage style that Games himself used, they showed a more up-market alternative to the solutions favoured by Penguin's rivals. Games devised a rigid structure and commissioned nine other designers to help create the required images (pp. 86–9). Titles appeared from April 1957 onwards, and the experiment lasted about a year until it was halted by Lane. The designs were described soon after as

*the first fully pictorial paperback covers in England with any kind of artistic integrity and a sense of adventure. The experiment was brought to an abrupt stop when the result on sales had proved inconclusive and the evidence of 'confusing the image' had become strong.*7

The experiment had been only half-heartedly carried out: no supporting publicity was produced to back up or explain the designs, and only twenty-nine designs actually appeared. Given the quality of most of the covers it seems an extraordinary waste – but they had broken the mould. During the following two years, John Curtis continued working as Art Director for covers. His layouts became less dependent on existing formulas and he started to employ younger freelance designers such as Derek Birdsall, Alan Fletcher and Herbert Spencer, who in turn used photography and more dynamic typography. The covers produced during this short period did not have the unity of the Games experiment, but they did point the way forward. A full-time cover art editor and a fresh approach to cover design were urgently needed.

OPPOSITE: During the 1950s Penguin faced increased competition from other paperback publishers. Penguin tried to steer a course which ensured that their books remained popular without looking cheap. As the decade progressed, dependence on the Gill Sans typeface diminished and the overall composition of the covers became less formal. Images – whether photographic or illustrative – were given a greater role in attracting the public, and while traditional observational illustration was used on many fiction titles, for the more serious Pelicans and Specials collage was increasingly used to express ideas.

Penguin by Design

Strategy for Survival

First Steps in Nuclear Disarmament

FABIAN

A Penguin Special by

WAYLAND YOUNG

2'6

Strategy for Survival, 1959.
Cover illustration by
Erwin Fabian.

Experimental layout by
Jan Tschichold, 1948 (assisted
by Erik Ellegaard Frederiksen).

Jan Tschichold's design reforms: the horizontal grid, 1948

Jan Tschichold's reforms did not involve a radical new look but rather a subtle facelift of all aspects of the cover designs, from the size, weight and position of each element of the typography to the drawing of the logo.

The most obvious change was the substitution of Gill Sans for Bodoni Ultra Bold in the publisher's name. Less noticeable to many, perhaps, was the care taken in optically letterspacing all text set in capital letters, both on the covers and inside the books. A comparison between *The Anatomy of Peace* (or the covers on pages 18–23) and the remainder of the covers on the following spread shows how much difference this makes. Initial versions of the redesign featured a fine line as a border to the orange panels, but this was dropped after a few titles. Tschichold also redrew Edward Young's 1939 version of the logo.

As with the pre-war covers, the horizontal grid was also adapted to allow for the inclusion of illustrations. *The Quatermass Experiment* (p. 59) is an early example of a 'TV tie-in'.

After the vertical grid appeared in 1951, the horizontal was only used occasionally for titles in the general list. One notable example was the suitably amended design for Penguin no. 1000, *One of Our Submarines* (p. 59), written by the firm's first production manager. Crime continued to use the horizontal grid until the early 1960s. The only alteration was in the typography, which was changed to a ranged-left arrangement and included a small amount of 'blurb'.

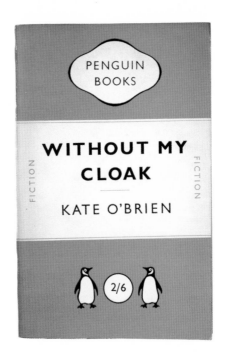

Without My Cloak, 1949.

Sailing, 1949.

The Anatomy of Peace, 1947.

The Romantic Exiles, 1949.

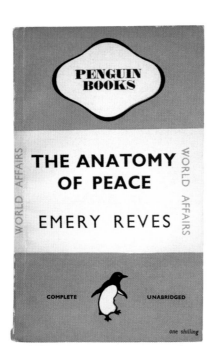

Sonia (dustjacket), 1949.

Charles Lamb and Elia, 1948.

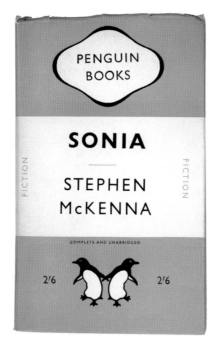

Penguin by Design

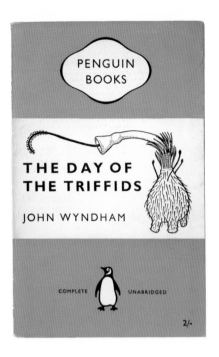

The Day of the Triffids, 1954.

The Quatermass Experiment, 1959.

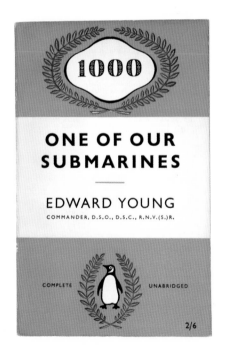

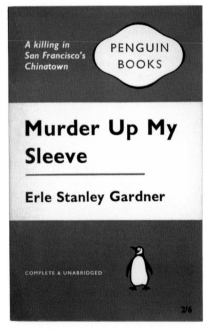

One of Our Submarines, 1954.

Murder Up My Sleeve, 1961.

Shakespeare, 1951

A Midsummer Night's Dream,
1940.

The first Shakespeare titles appeared in 1938 and were typographically undistinguished. When the series was resumed it offered Jan Tschichold the opportunity to make far-reaching changes both to the cover and to the text setting inside. His assistant Erik Ellegaard Frederiksen wrote later:

The Penguin Shakespeare was probably the series that had been most neglected typographically. The cover was red and plain; the typography set in Times with semi-bold headlines. Tschichold let Reynolds Stone, one of England's most distinguished wood engravers, cut a portrait of Shakespeare to which Tschichold cut a frame with beautiful typography. With red type above and below the portrait, it is one the most beautiful of Tschichold's works. The type in the text itself was set in Bembo, and the title was also adorned with a square Stone portrait. The paper for this edition is wood-free, and a little thicker than that used for the normal Penguins. The paper colour was also altered to a comfortable, light yellow tone, and the combination of the paper mass was altered. The Penguin Shakespeare was unrecognizable. The Sonnets – a dream assignment – were included in the series, and thus one could buy this classic in an elegant paperback edition. (Frederiksen, pp. 16–17)

Twelfth Night (back cover),
1968.

Tschichold returned to Switzerland, but this cover design continued to be used until 1967. The heavy uncoated cover board originally used was eventually replaced by standard smooth art board, which had much less visual and tactile appeal.

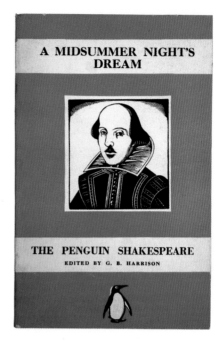

Penguin by Design

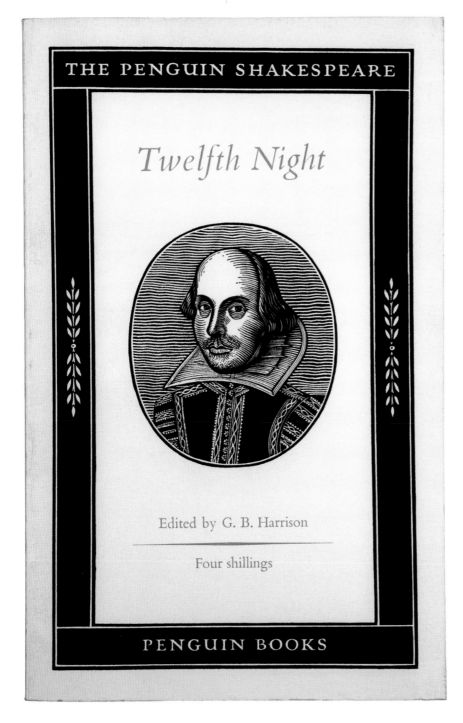

Pelicans redesigned, 1949

An Outline of European Architecture, 1951.

The Pelican redesign begun by Tschichold involved a departure from the original horizontal grid and would later be reflected in his designs for poetry and Shakespeare and in Hans Schmoller's designs for the handbooks.

A frame carried the imprint within each side. This allowed an area for differing treatments of text and the incorporation of an image when appropriate.

The central panel of many books was purely typographic and sometimes included text describing the contents. Pelicans remained related to the main series by their use of Gill Sans but differed from those titles by using – nearly always – upper and lower case instead of capitals only.

Covers could also feature illustrations, the styles of which were very carefully considered to reflect each title's content.

A later refinement to this design was to enlarge the frame to accommodate all the text and to entirely surround an illustration (*Grasses*).

Grasses, 1954. [Cover illustration by Joan Sampson.]

Penguin by Design

The Earth Beneath Us, 1958.
Cover illustration by
Reinganum.

A PELICAN BOOK

A PELICAN BOOK

A PELICAN BOOK

H. H. SWINNERTON

The Earth Beneath Us

The origin, age, and
formation of the earth and the
start of life upon it

A PELICAN BOOK

5/-

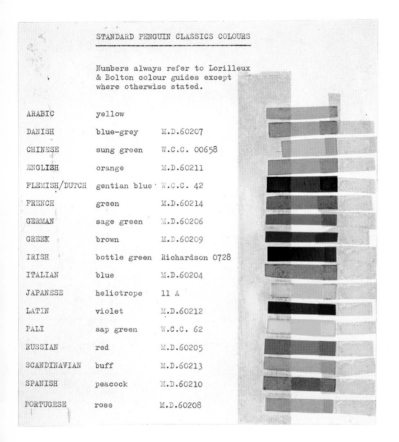

STANDARD PENGUIN CLASSICS COLOURS

Numbers always refer to Lorilleux & Bolton colour guides except where otherwise stated.

ARABIC	yellow	
DANISH	blue-grey	M.D.60207
CHINESE	sung green	W.C.C. 00658
ENGLISH	orange	M.D.60211
FLEMISH/DUTCH	gentian blue	W.C.C. 42
FRENCH	green	M.D.60214
GERMAN	sage green	M.D.60206
GREEK	brown	M.D.60209
IRISH	bottle green	Richardson 0728
ITALIAN	blue	M.D.60204
JAPANESE	heliotrope	11 A
LATIN	violet	M.D.60212
PALI	sap green	W.C.C. 62
RUSSIAN	red	M.D.60205
SCANDINAVIAN	buff	M.D.60213
SPANISH	peacock	M.D.60210
PORTUGESE	rose	M.D.60208

The Classics colour palette.

Classics restyled, 1947

The Classics series was one of the first to benefit from Jan Tschichold's attention, and, as with the standard horizontal grid, his changes were about refinement.

While all the key elements of John Overton's original design (p. 47) were retained, Tschichold made four small changes and in doing so presented the cover as a simpler, more balanced composition. The colour of the roundel and patterned border was changed to black, making the cover two-colour not three; the type panel was enlarged to accommodate the roundel; the series title was incorporated in the panel, with a swelled rule to separate it from the translator; and a more delicately patterned border was used.

The design of the roundels was given to a number of different illustrators. Credits for the designs were given in the books themselves only towards the end of the 1950s. In some cases in-house staff traced over photographs of ancient coins. A selection of the roundels is shown overleaf.

A couple of titles do not adhere to the norm: *Faust, Part 1* (L12), a pre-Tschichold design, has the roundel on the dustjacket only (the cover itself is plain brown), and Plutarch's *Fall of the Roman Republic* (L84), although originally written in Greek, is purple.

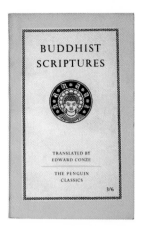

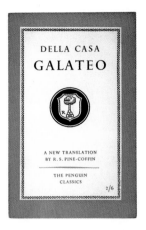

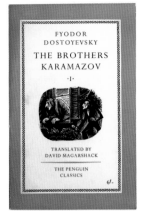

Buddhist Scriptures, 1960. [Roundel artwork by Elizabeth Friedlander.]

Galateo, 1958. [Roundel artwork by Elizabeth Friedlander.]

The Brothers Karamazov, Volume 1, 1958. [Roundel artwork by Cecil Keeling.]

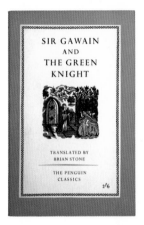

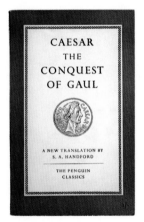

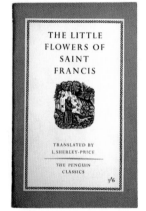

Sir Gawain and the Green Knight, 1959.

The Conquest of Gaul, 1951.

The Little Flower of Saint Francis, 1959. [Wood engraving by Reynolds Stone.]

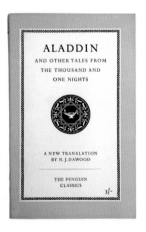

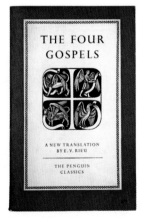

Three Tales (Flaubert), 1961.

Aladdin, 1960.

The Four Gospels, 1952. [Wood engraving by Reynolds Stone.]

1. *Against Nature*, 1959.

2. *The Persian Expedition*, 1949.

3. *Alexander the Great*, 1958.
[Diana Bloomfield.]

4. *Candide*, 1947.
[William Grimmond.]

5. *Faust, Part 1*, 1949.
[Dorrit Wayne.]

6. *The Odyssey*, 1959.
[Elizabeth Friedlander.]

7. *Essays* (Montaigne), 1958.

8. *The Canterbury Tales*, 1951.
[Based on a woodcut in Wynkyn
de Worde's 1498 edition.]

9. *Five Plays* (Molière), 1953.
[Elizabeth Friedlander.]

10. *Germinal*, 1954. [Dennis Hall.]

11. *The Golden Ass*, 1950.

12. *The History of the English
Church*, 1955.
[Elizabeth Friedlander.]

13. *The Iliad*, 1950.
[George Buday.]

14. *The Imitation of Christ*, 1952.
[Elizabeth Friedlander.]

15. *The Jewish War*, 1959.
[Berthold Wolpe.]

16. *Gargantua and Pantagruel*,
1955. [Roy Morgan.]

17. *The Idiot*, 1955.
[John Diebel.]

18. *Don Quixote*, 1950.
[William Grimmond.]

19. *The Koran*, 1956.
[Mrs A. Janssens.]

20. *The Ladder of Perfection*, 1957.

21. *The Last Days of Socrates*,
1954. [Also used on L68 and L194.]

22. *The Acts of the Apostles*, 1957.
[Elizabeth Friedlander.]

23. *The Mountain Inn*, 1955.
[David Gentleman.]

24. *Njal's Saga*, 1960.
[Elizabeth Friedlander.]

25. *The Oresteian Trilogy*, 1956.

26. *The Pastoral Poems*, 1949.
[William Grimmond.]

27. *The Peloponnesian War*, 1954.
[Elizabeth Friedlander.]

28. *Boule de Suif*, 1946.
[Clarke Hutton.]

29. *The Seagull*, 1954.

30. *On Britain and Germany*, 1948.
[William Grimmond.]

31. *The Thousand and One Nights*,
1955.

32. *Three Plays* (Ibsen), 1950.

33. *The Voyage of Argo*, 1959.

34. *The Lusiads*, 1952.
[Elizabeth Friedlander.]

35. *War and Peace*, Volume 1, 1957.
[Elizabeth Friedlander.]

36. *The Theban Plays*, 1947.
[Bert Pugh.]

Music scores, 1949

The idea of pocket-sized music scores at a
popular price was novel, but the potential
market relatively small, and the sales outlets appropriate for them were not the
same as those for Penguin's other books.
Nevertheless, over seven years thirty titles
were published, but when the series
ceased to earn money it was dropped.

The list was edited by the composer
Gordon Jacob and covered the most
popular titles heard in concert halls and
available on record. They had the advantage of being out of copyright.

Designed for a horizontal version of
the larger B size by Jan Tschichold, they
are highly regarded both as miniature
scores and for their elegant covers. Each
features a patterned background reminiscent of the endpapers of an old hardback book. The typography appears
in a formal, bordered panel and is set in
Garamond, with its decorative italic being
used for the title itself.

Some of the patterns were later used
by Hans Schmoller for his redesign of the
Penguin Poets series in 1954 (p. 71), and
later still by Germano Facetti for his version of the poetry covers in 1966 (p.146).

Overtures (Mozart), 1951.
[Cover design by Hans Schmoller.
Pattern re-used in different colours
for poetry series: D30, 33, 36, 45,
47, 50 and 57.]

Penguin by Design

MOZART

*Overtures: The Magic Flute
and Don Giovanni*

PENGUIN SCORES 15 · 3/-

Poetry, 1948 and 1954

Robert Burns, 1947.

The Penguin Poets series first appeared in 1941, but only three titles (*Robert Burns* was no. 3, in 1946) had been published before Tschichold's arrival at Penguin. He gave the series a bordered cover design (*C. Day Lewis*) in 1948, featuring Garamond Italic for the author's name.

In 1954 the design for the series was revised again, this time by Hans Schmoller. This design owed much to that of the music scores (previous spread), and several of the titles used patterns from that series printed in different colours. The author's name is again in italic, but in the much wider Walbaum; Schmoller's previous employers, the Curwen Press, had been the first to use this typeface in Britain in 1925.

For some authors, the monogram identifier used on their main series titles was incorporated into their poetry cover (*Hilaire Belloc*).

C. Day Lewis, 1951.

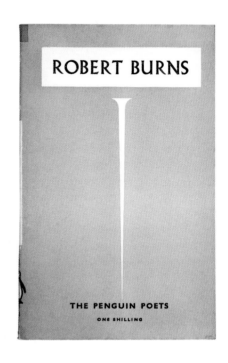

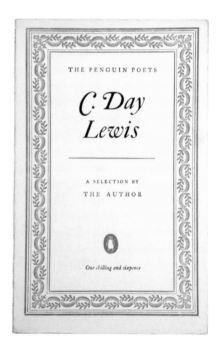

Penguin by Design

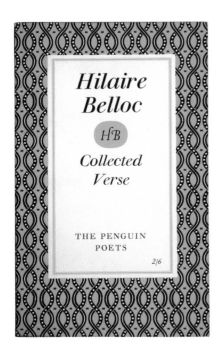

Hilaire Belloc, 1958.

Swinburne, 1961.

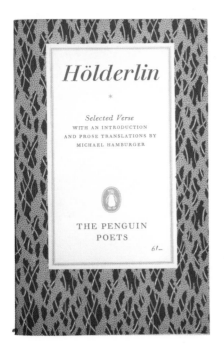

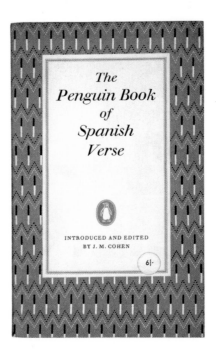

Hölderlin, 1961.

The Penguin Book of Spanish Verse, 1960.

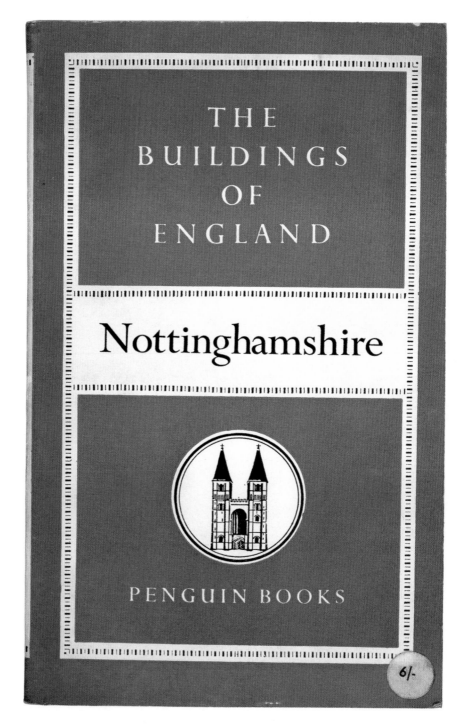

THE
BUILDINGS
OF
ENGLAND

Nottinghamshire

PENGUIN BOOKS

6/-

Buildings of England, 1951

Nikolaus Pevsner had suggested the idea
of a series of architectural guides to other
publishers before the war, but it was
not taken up. Having been drawn into
Penguin during the war, he suggested the
idea to Allen Lane and was encouraged
to work on both the guides and another
proposal: a Pelican history of art.

Pevsner's personal touring of each
county was aided by notes provided by
researchers who had worked for up to a
year in advance. His own observations
were then written up each evening, keeping the whole work fresh. This ambitious
task took twenty-three years to complete
and needed many collaborators along
the way. As early as 1954, and despite
great critical acclaim, it was not making
money, and sponsorship was needed if
the series was to continue. In addition to
Pevsner waiving his royalty, grants from
the Leverhulme Trust were instrumental
in the completion of the series. Further
smaller grants came from ABC Television and Arthur Guinness & Sons Ltd.

In appearance, the volumes were presented in a neo-classical style similar to
the Classics (p. 65). The typeface is again
Eric Gill's Perpetua, and a roundel –
based on a photograph within the book
– is also a feature.

The first titles appeared as paperbacks, and in 1952 these were given the
added protection of a dustjacket of identical design. That same year hardback
editions began to appear. These featured
a different dustjacket, initially retaining
the roundel, but from 1953 they featured
a black and white cut-out photograph
on a green background.

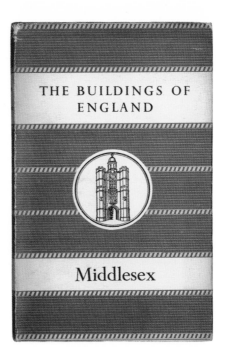

Middlesex (dustjacket), 1951.

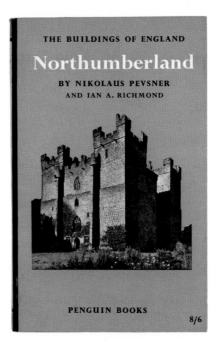

Northumberland (dustjacket),
1957.

Handbooks in the fifties

The Penguin Knitting Book,
1957. Cover design by Heather
Standring.

Handbooks first appeared in wartime,
with titles associated with the war effort
such as *Soft Fruit Growing* and *Rabbit
Farming*. Initially numbered as Specials,
they became a separate named series
from 1943 onwards.

By the mid 1950s Hans Schmoller
had given them a distinctive cover design
which featured a border filled with illustrations. These could be representational
or abstract. On these standard designs
the typography followed a set pattern
and was in the regular and italic variants
of Gill Sans. Occasionally (*The Game
of Chess*) the logo itself could be drawn
into the design.

For certain subjects, more distinctive
illustrations were commissioned. In
these, every element of the standard
design, except the idea of a border surrounding the central 'type' area, was
open to manipulation.

Soft Fruit Growing, 1951.

Penguin by Design

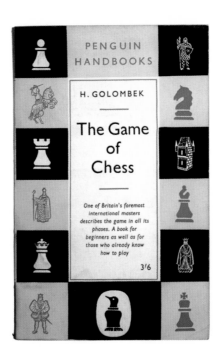

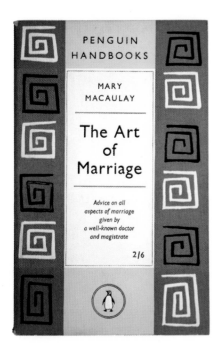

Paint Your Own Pictures, 1954.

The Game of Chess, 1959.

The Art of Marriage, 1957.

Plats du Jour, 1958.
Cover illustration by
David Gentleman.

King Penguins under
Hans Schmoller

When King Penguins first appeared in
1939 it was as small collectable hard-
backs, and the series covered an eclectic
range of subjects (pp. 26–7). The series
continued throughout the 1950s with
Hans Schmoller as Art Director. As
before, the cover designs are unified not
by any particular 'look', but by a sensitivity to the material reproduced within,
which was carefully reflected through
appropriate typography, illustration or
photography.

As well as having an overview of the
series, Schmoller was directly involved
as the designer of several titles, including the formal – almost nostalgic –
John Speed's Atlas of England & Wales,
as well as the more contemporary
Sculpture of the Parthenon.

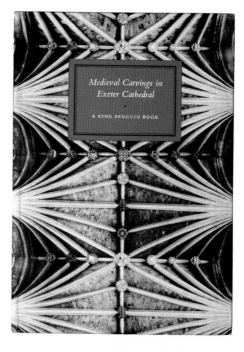

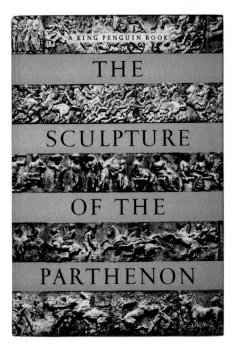

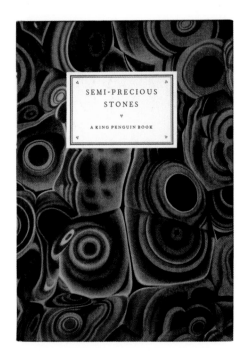

The vertical grid, 1951

The Illustrated Classics covers (pp. 24–5) can be seen as precursors to the vertical grid, which may have made its first appearance on dustjackets for books with covers in the horizontal style as early as 1948. From roughs in the Penguin archive in Bristol, it is apparent that this vertical grid was being worked on within months of Tschichold finally perfecting Edward Young's horizontal grid. Begun by Tschichold with his assistant Erik Ellegaard Frederiksen, several variations were explored before it was resolved by Hans Schmoller. This design ensured continuity with the earlier Penguin standard design through its three divisions and use of colour. The central area was most commonly used for simple line illustrations but could also contain an extract from a book review or some 'blurb'. The first title with the vertical grid itself did not appear until 1952 – Synge's *Collected Plays*.

With only a few exceptions, such as Edward Young's *One of Our Submarines* (p. 59), fiction adopted this design, but the crime series – apart from the Games designs (pp. 86–9) – continued almost exclusively with the horizontal grid until 1962.

OPPOSITE AND LEFT: Experimental layouts by Jan Tschichold, 1948 (assisted by Erik Ellegaard Frederiksen).

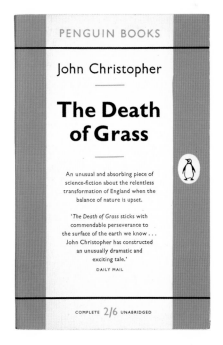

The Death of Grass, 1958.

The Greek Myths, Volume 1, 1955.

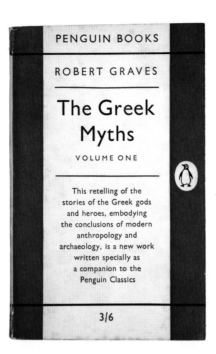

PENGUIN BOOKS

ROBERT GRAVES

The Greek Myths

VOLUME ONE

This retelling of the
stories of the Greek gods
and heroes, embodying
the conclusions of modern
anthropology and
archaeology, is a new work
written specially as
a companion to the
Penguin Classics

3/6

The vertical grid: author identities

As the decade progressed, other fonts
began to appear on covers as a way of
giving particular authors their own
limited identity.

The Corvinus typeface (designed by
Imre Reiner between 1929 and 1934)
was used for Aldous Huxley from 1951
and marked the very first departure from
Gill Sans on a fiction cover.

For other authors, a monogram or
other symbol was devised. The most
lavish of these was the phoenix and
flames for D. H. Lawrence. This design
would become the best known of all the
author identifiers after Penguin successfully defended their publication of an un-
expurgated edition of *Lady Chatterley's
Lover* in the High Court in 1960 and it
went on to sell 3 million copies.

Over My Dead Body, 1955.

PENGUIN BOOKS

Over
My Dead
Body

REX
STOUT

—

*A Crime Club
Choice*

COMPLETE 2/6 UNABRIDGED

80

Penguin by Design

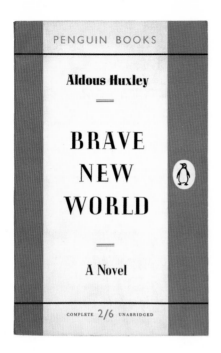

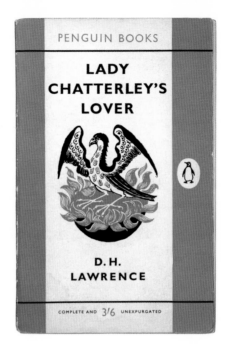

Brave New World, 1955.

Lady Chatterley's Lover, 1960. [Phoenix redrawn by Stephen Russ.]

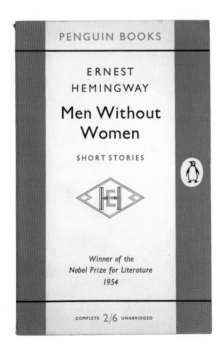

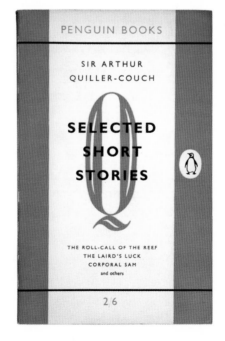

Men Without Women, 1955.

Selected Short Stories, 1957.

The vertical grid:
integration of illustration

The New Men, 1959. Cover
illustration by Erwin Fabian.

The vertical grid layout was designed for, and worked well with, illustrations of a simple kind, but as time went by the illustrations grew larger and were allowed to invade the flanking orange borders.

    After the initial designs featuring single-colour illustrations, it is possible to see in the evolution of these covers a gradual gnawing away at the fixed attitudes which had dominated Penguin practice and which Allen Lane held as sacrosanct. The principal changes are illustrated here and on the following spread.

    The first steps towards a greater graphic freedom involved a careful encroachment on the border (*The Pajama Game*). Another attempt to add variety saw illustrations that integrated the type in some way (*The Seeds of Time* and *The Black Cloud*).

Edmund Campion, 1957. Cover
illustration by Derrick Harris.

    Commercial pressures dictated that cinema and television were taken advantage of whenever possible. Frequently this meant the use of photography. Integrating this within the confines of the vertical grid was not always satisfactory (*Breakfast at Tiffany's*) or possible (*The Contenders*). Inevitably, full-cover images eventually appeared for a small number of titles (*The Cruel Sea*).

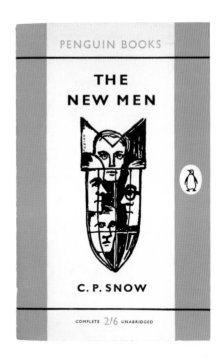

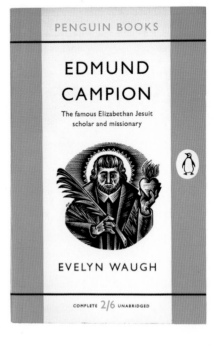

Penguin by Design

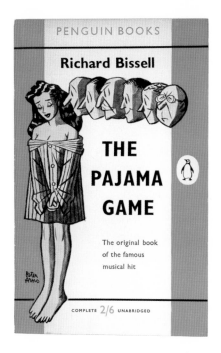

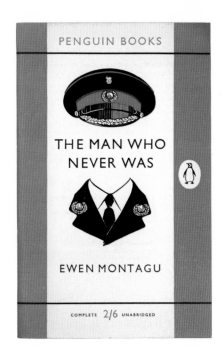

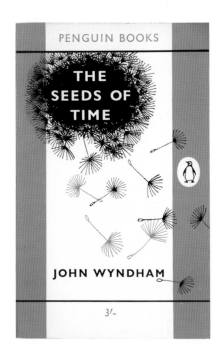

The Pajama Game, 1958.
Cover illustration by Peter Arno.

The Man Who Never Was, 1956.

The Seeds of Time, 1963.
Cover drawing by John Griffiths.

The Black Cloud, 1960.
Cover design by John Griffiths.

Penguin Science Fiction, 1961.
Cover illustration by Brian Keogh.

The Contenders, 1962.
Cover photograph from the Radio
Times Hulton Picture Library.

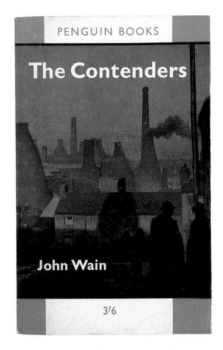

Breakfast at Tiffany's, 1961.
[The cover shows Audrey
Hepburn in Blake Edwards' film
Breakfast at Tiffany's.]

The Misfits, 1961.
Marilyn Monroe, Clark Gable,
and Montgomery Clift in a scene
from the Seven Artists Production
released through United Artists.

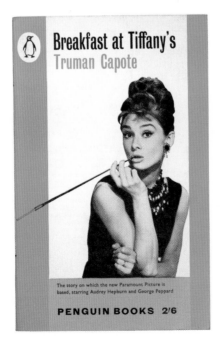

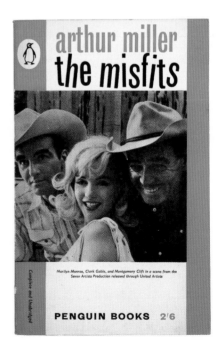

Penguin by Design

The Great Escape, 1957. Cover
illustration by Abram Games.

PAUL BRICKHILL

THE GREAT ESCAPE

PENGUIN BOOKS 2/6

The Abram Games
cover experiment, 1957–8

Facing growing competition, Penguin carried out an experiment to see what effect full-colour covers would have on sales. Hans Schmoller invited Abram Games to be Art Director of the project.

Games established a simple grid which provided a 1 1/4-inch panel for the author, title and logo above a clear area containing the illustration. The publisher's name was at the foot of the cover, overprinted or reversed-out of the illustration. The type used was the regular and extra bold weights of Gill Sans, and the logo sat on a panel coloured orange for fiction, green for crime or magenta for non-fiction.

Games was responsible for commissioning other illustrators to provide covers, and nine did so during the life of the project. To Games's dismay the company did not promote the covers in any way, and some of the public did not believe they were Penguins at all. Less than thirty covers had appeared before Allen Lane decided to stop the experiment on the grounds that the extra expense of the full-colour printing was not offset by an increase in sales.

The Big Show, 1958. Cover illustration by David Caplan.

Flames in the Sky, 1958. Cover illustration by Abram Games.

Tibetan Marches, 1957. Cover
illustration by Stanley Godsell.

Tappan's Burro, 1958. Cover
illustration by Dennis Bailey.

My Uncle Silas, 1958.
[Cover illustration by Edward
Ardizzone.]

The Song of the Whip, 1957.
Cover illustration by
Abram Games.

Penguin by Design

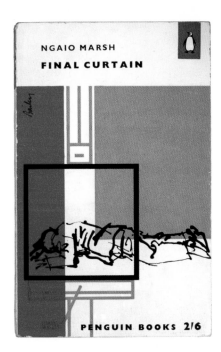

The Case of the Drowning Duck,
1957. Cover illustration by
Hans Unger.

Final Curtain, 1958. Cover
illustration by Dennis Bailey.

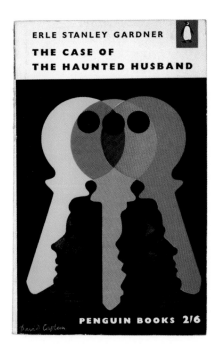

The Case of the Haunted
Husband, 1957. Cover
illustration by David Caplan.

The Tiger in the Smoke, 1957.
Cover design by David Caplan.

II. Consistency and Competition, 1947–59

89

John Curtis as temporary Art Director, 1957–9

Nijinsky, 1960.
The drawing of Nijinsky on the cover is taken from a poster by Jean Cocteau painted in 1909.

Despite the failure of the Games experiment, Penguin covers continued to evolve. John Curtis, Publicity Manager since 1952, took over as temporary cover Art Director from 1957 to 1959.

As well as working with illustrators such as David Gentleman (who had first been commissioned to work for Penguin by Hans Schmoller), Curtis was instrumental in commissioning covers from younger designers such as Derek Birdsall (later to form Omnific) and Alan Fletcher, Colin Forbes and Bob Gill (who became Fletcher/Forbes/Gill and, later, Pentagram).

For certain titles, such as those in the Biography series, Curtis encouraged a departure from the dominant designs of stripes and borders and allowed a much freer use of elements on the cover. For a series of illustrated books aimed at a younger audience (which were at one point going to be called Picture Pelicans) he commissioned more radical covers with a strong use of white, and bold typography to match the quality of the illustration.

The Diaghilev Ballet, 1909–1929, 1960. The illustration on the cover is taken from a drawing by Jean Cocteau.

Curtis's art direction was most notable on the Pelican series. The imprint and logo were reduced to a strip at the foot of the cover and the remainder could be designed afresh for each title. The illustrative element of these covers shows a fascination with printing processes, overprinting, reversing-out, and even the power of the white cover board itself. And for the first time on a Penguin book, the typography was allowed to be expressive and suggestive rather than simply readable and/or beautiful.

OPPOSITE: *Artificial Satellites*, 1960. Cover design by John Griffiths.

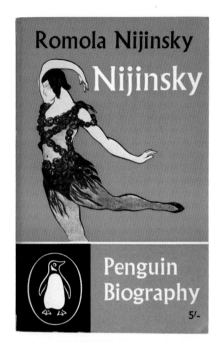

ARTIFICIAL SATELLITES

A picture guide to rockets, satellites, and space probes

MICHAEL W. OVENDEN

A Penguin Book 5s

Applied Geography, 1961.
Cover design by Juliet Renny.

Archaeology from the Earth,
1961. Cover design by Bruce
Robertson.

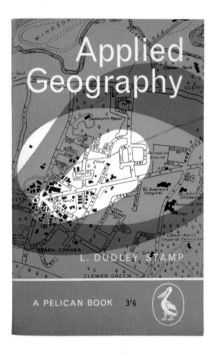

Geology and Scenery, 1961.
Cover design by Kenneth
Rowland.

*The Social Psychology of
Industry*, 1962. Cover design by
Derek Birdsall.

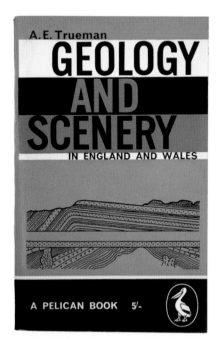

Penguin by Design

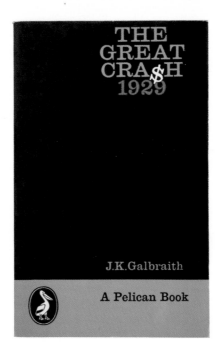

Ethics, 1961.
Cover design by Robin Fior.

The Great Crash 1929, 1971.
Cover design by Derek Birdsall.

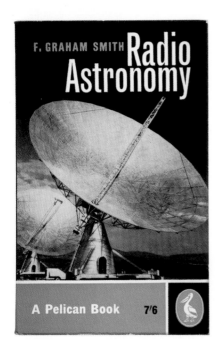

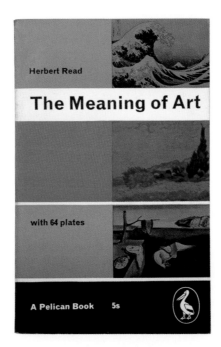

Radio Astronomy, 1960.

The Meaning of Art, 1961.
Cover design by Herbert Spencer.

BELOW: Composite of artwork taken from *The Case of the Drowning Duck*, 1966 (p. 136), and *The Case of the Curious Bride*, 1966. Illustrations by Giannetto Coppola.

III. Art Direction and Graphic Design, 1960–70

III. Art Direction and Graphic Design, 1960–70

The Arup and Dowson building

An Outline of European Architecture, 1961. Jacket design by Eugen O. Sporer, Munich (255 × 220 mm).

Penguin's Silver Jubilee publication, *Penguins Progress, 1935–1960*, captured the company at a turning point. Partly descriptive of the company's activities and partly another pat on the back, it is fundamentally reflective and shows little concern for what was to come. While the period from 1947 to 1959 can be seen as one centred on improving standards and ensuring consistency, the following decade was almost all about change. There were changes of opinion within the company about how it should meet the challenge of an increasingly competitive market and there were fundamental changes which affected the status of the company itself.

Penguin became a public company when it was floated on the London Stock Exchange on 20 April 1961.[1] Allen Lane continued as Chairman and Managing Director, but his hands-on involvement would be intermittent during this, the last decade of his life. He did take a great interest in the expansion of the warehouse space, for which the company commissioned leading architects Ove Arup and Philip Dowson. Building began in 1964, the first of several on-site expansions during this time. The site was closed in 2004 (see Chapter V) and is currently being cleared for redevelopment.

The one constant throughout the decade was the quality of Penguin's text design, still guided by Hans Schmoller, who was made a Director in 1960. Working in a traditional (in all the best senses of the word) manner, he had long come out of Tschichold's shadow and was universally respected for the quality and sensitivity of his designs. He revised the *Penguin Composition Rules*, thereby influencing all the printers who worked for the company (and thus, no doubt, typographical standards across the industry). For many people, the design which best exemplified his mastery of controlling complicated textual variations was the one-volume Pelican Shakespeare, a co-edition between Allen Lane The Penguin Press (p. 100) and Pelican in 1969.

During the 1960s the development of new typesetting methods allowed radical changes to take place. Hot-metal typesetting and letterpress printing (with its distinctive depth of ink and physical impression) eventually gave way to various forms of phototypesetting and offset-litho printing. With letterpress, illustrated books were generally printed on two kinds of paper, and text and images appear in discrete sections. The earlier volumes of the Pelican History of Art typify this approach (while Penguin's lavish Jubilee Edition of Nikolaus Pevsner's *An Outline of European Architecture*, designed in-house at Prestel Verlag and printed in Germany in 1960, is a notable exception).

The use of phototypesetting and offset-litho printing brought costs down dramatically, and, because it was easier to print both text and images on one paper stock, their integration became far easier and more cost-effective. Designers such as Jerry Cinamon, initially commissioned to design covers for Pelicans, worked under Schmoller on internal book design. Cinamon joined the staff in 1965 and in 1966 was given the task of redesigning the Pelican History of Art as A5-sized integrated paperbacks. This was followed by the Style and Civilization series and Pelican architectural titles, among others.

If Schmoller and the text designers represented continuity through the 1960s, then Tony Godwin represented change. Appointed initially as an editorial advisor by Allen Lane in May 1960, Tony Godwin was the mercurial manager of Better Books, Bumpus and the City Bookshop. Within a short period of time he became Fiction Editor, then Chief Editor. Godwin was a rigorous editor with far-ranging interests, but he also brought to the company an intimate knowledge of what happened at the point of sale. Editorially, he believed that Penguin, in common with other paperback publishers, was relying too heavily on the work of the previous sixty years and that more-radical editorial policies should be pursued in order to nurture new and emerging talent. In terms of selling books, he recognized that if the company was going to keep up with developments in graphic design generally it would need a different kind of designer from either Hans Schmoller or John Curtis, and new designs would need to be introduced, not piecemeal, but as part of a comprehensive policy of revamping the company's image.

When the Abram Games full-colour cover experiment had appeared in 1957, Godwin, not then on the Penguin staff, had criticized the covers for being 'dressed far above their station in life'.[2] Now at Penguin, Godwin wanted covers which addressed the marketplace far more directly, and for a full-time Cover Art Director he turned to a designer of a younger generation, Germano Facetti, whose approach was cerebral rather than literal.

Facetti, who began working at Penguin in January 1961, was born in 1926 and, having worked in Milan for Banfi, Belgiojoso, Peressutti & Rogers, first came to Britain in 1950. During this period he attended Ed Wright's evening classes in typography at the Central School of Arts & Crafts, worked with Theo Crosby and Ed Wright on the entrance area of the 'This is Tomorrow' exhibition at the Whitechapel Art Gallery (1956) and designed 'integrated books' for the publisher Rathbone. He then moved to Paris, where he worked as an interior designer for the marketing arm of the Snip advertising agency and also helped set up the Snark International Picture Library.

Tony Godwin

2. Quoted in Aynsley and Lloyd Jones, p. 121.

Germano Facetti

Romek Marber

Facetti found Penguin had many categories of books whose appearance was quite disparate; often, the use of the relevant logo was the only unifying device. Part of the cause was undoubtedly that Penguin had grown to huge proportions: new titles and reissues were appearing at the rate of seventy a month, and each demanded a freshly designed cover. Facetti's job was to transform them into something contemporary while retaining continuity.

Facetti used traditional Penguin colours to reassert the identity of the company, to strengthen its image and to ensure some link with the past; but his fundamental impact was in changing the covers through a more defined use of illustration, collage and photography. The first series to be given a comprehensive revision was the green crime series in 1961 (pp. 102–6). Three designers – Brian Sewell, Derek Birdsall and Romek Marber (who had not designed for Penguin before) – had been asked to submit suggestions, and Marber's solution was adopted. His initial designs were accompanied by two sheets of handwritten analysis of the existing (three stripes) design and his own proposals. It is worth quoting extensively from these, both for their clarity of thought and because the rational approach behind them underpins much of Facetti's subsequent work at Penguin.

Current covers (impact and efficiency)

the current constant typographic covers in present-day paperback publishing have no means to excite or attract attention. With the addition each year of new titles to the Penguin Crime list it becomes difficult just by looking at the current typographic cover to discern between books already bought and those newly published.

New covers (impact and efficiency)

… the typography will remain constant, and the variation which will occur is dictated by the length of the titles. This arrangement and the change in the colour of the type, between the title and the name of the author, will help the public to recognize with ease either the title or name of the author, whichever happens to interest them.

The pictorial idea, be it drawing, collage or photograph, will indicate the atmospheric content of the book. The public's awareness of kinematic images offers the Crime series, particularly, great photographic possibilities. The clarity and simplicity of the pictorial idea will emphasize the contrast between covers, will be easily memorized, and will have – when books are displayed in large numbers – a cumulative effect.

Penguin by Design

To retain the Penguin identity, these formal elements are translated into a 'grid'. This grid, which will form the basic structure for the design of all Crime covers, will also help in the problem of production.[3]

3. See Spencer ('Penguin Covers: A Correction'), p. 62.

The advantage of this grid was immediately apparent to Facetti. Marber was commissioned to design twenty crime covers a year, and Richard Hollis, Birdsall, Bruce Robertson, Edwin Taylor and F. H. K. Henrion also contributed designs. The grid itself was then used by Facetti on fiction covers and Pelicans, and was eventually applied to the Penguin Modern Classics. Other series appeared with variants of the grid.

A similar horizontal division of space was used by Facetti in his redesign of the Penguin Classics (pp. 124–5). This series had been a huge success since its launch in 1946. The initial selling point was that it brought contemporary English translations of great works to a wide audience at low cost; the titles' subsequent adoption on to university reading lists provided confirmation of their scholarship. But after nearly twenty years their appearance could be thought old-fashioned. Under Facetti they now received a photographic treatment, and, in keeping with everything else, sans serif typography.

During this period too, Penguin Specials were reinvigorated, with subjects reflecting the concerns of the era: membership of the Common Market (as it was then known), space exploration, transport and social issues (pp. 112–15). Although the covers tended to have very direct and expressive graphic imagery, a consistent use of sans serif typefaces, a colour palette of red and black on white, and intelligent use of space showed the series to be clearly integral to the new Penguin look.

Part of the success of the Facetti approach lay in his choice of other designers. All those mentioned above were slightly younger than Facetti at the outset of their careers and had a similar starting point, which might be described as a non-doctrinaire and flexible approach to modernism. This consensus of outlook ensured a continuity of feel across many of the series despite considerable differences in detail.

After a number of years, Tony Godwin felt that the new designs for the fiction covers were not as successful as they ought to be and decided that a separate Fiction Art Editor was needed. His first instinct had been to appoint a well-known American designer such as Milton Glaser, but over a drink one day Alan Aldridge suggested himself as Art Director to the list and he got the job. Aldridge took up the post in March 1965, and his responsibilities included crime and science fiction titles but excluded Modern Classics and the

Alan Aldridge

The Penguin Book of Comics, 1967. Cover illustration by Bob Smithers.

4. The name deliberately mirrored 'Uncle John's' company, John Lane The Bodley Head, and by a happy coincidence Lane was able to acquire the same Vigo Street address where he began his own career with The Bodley Head.

English Library. His office was not at Harmondsworth but with the editorial offices in John Street in the Holborn area of London.

Aldridge was first and foremost an illustrator. He had attended the Graphics Workshop on Conduit Street run by Bob Gill and Lou Klein, and had been given occasional freelance work by Facetti as well as working in the *Sunday Times* magazine studio. He had a view of cover design quite different from Facetti's, believing that a cover should attract attention by whatever means. His own work showed a mix of comic, art nouveau and pop art influences, and he frequently employed photography. He also wrote *The Penguin Book of Comics* (1967, with George Perry) and *The Butterfly Ball and Grasshopper's Feast* (1973, with William Plomer).

Briefed by Godwin and the other editors, Aldridge offered the complete cover area to the designers he commissioned. Photography, hand-lettering, decorative typefaces and montage were all used, the only firm constant being a large Penguin logo in the corner. They represented a significant shift from the old style of narrative illustration favoured in the 1950s, and were quite different from the knowing references favoured by Facetti. The title had become more important than the publisher. Ultimately, success was often down to the sensitivity of the individual designer: at their best, the covers caught your eye and made you think; at their worst you learnt more about the designer than the book or its author.

Alan Aldridge's cover designs won fans and created enemies in equal measure, with many booksellers and authors among the latter. Their criticisms helped fuel in Allen Lane a growing resentment towards Tony Godwin. The disagreement led to silences rather than open warfare, with Lane fearing a *coup d'état* and Godwin perhaps feeling that he had over-reached himself within the company. Another cause of friction between them was the lacklustre launch of Penguin's new hardback imprint – Allen Lane The Penguin Press.4 Preparations were far hastier than Godwin had wanted, and while the books' designs were exemplary, it took some time for editorial policy to stabilize.

Matters with Godwin came to a head after he commissioned the cartoonist Siné's *Massacre* and some booksellers refused to stock the title because of its violent and sexual content (pp. 140–41). Boardroom unrest continued until Lane reasserted his authority one last time and Godwin left, 'by mutual consent', in May 1967.

Alan Aldridge also left in the wake of Godwin's departure, and thus the fiction list was temporarily without an Art Director. In the ensuing uncertainty a

Penguin by Design

decision was taken to insert the words A PENGUIN BOOK in 36-point Optima at the top of all front covers regardless of the design below – a panic measure to re-establish Penguin's identity. If stability and direction were to be regained, new blood was urgently required.

Penguin found it in May 1968. At the suggestion of the editor Oliver Caldecott, David Pelham was appointed Fiction Art Director. Before his appointment, Pelham had been commissioned as a freelance to design some covers. Lane had been impressed by Pelham's exposition of these and for the first six months of Pelham's tenure took a renewed interest in cover design, discussing each with him personally.

David Pelham

David Pelham had studied at St Martin's School of Art in London, leaving in 1958 and then working for *Ambassador*, *Studio International* and *Harper's Bazaar* before joining Penguin. The experience of working with and commissioning a wide range of illustrators, designers and photographers made him a far more accomplished Art Director than Aldridge. Pelham decided that to retain the company's identity he need only introduce a minimal grid with a consistent spine and back cover treatment, and a virtually blank canvas for the front with a logo appearing in a set size in one corner. Where Facetti had used people of a similar outlook to himself to design covers, Pelham was prepared to take a far more catholic approach, and he commissioned designs which ranged from the directly illustrative to ones which allowed for an author identity independent of content. Stylistically these might embrace photographic collages, drawings and American-style 'retro' images.

By 1969 Allen Lane had been in publishing for fifty years, a fact celebrated by the publication of James Joyce's *Ulysses* as Penguin no. 3000 (pp. 158–9). Further public recognition of his contribution to the industry came when he was made a Companion of Honour in the Queen's Birthday Honours list. By this point, however, Lane was increasingly concerned about his health and about the succession of the company. Despite having a larger list of published titles covering a wider range of subjects than any of its rivals, Penguin still had insufficient working capital, leaving it a potential target for a takeover bid. In order to avert this possibility, and shortly before being diagnosed with cancer, Allen Lane opened negotiations for the sale of the company to Longman, a British company with which Penguin had been working closely for some years. Longman was taken over by Pearson during negotiations, and it was to Pearson Longman that Penguin Books Ltd was eventually sold for £15 million on 21 August 1970, shortly after Lane's death on 7 July.

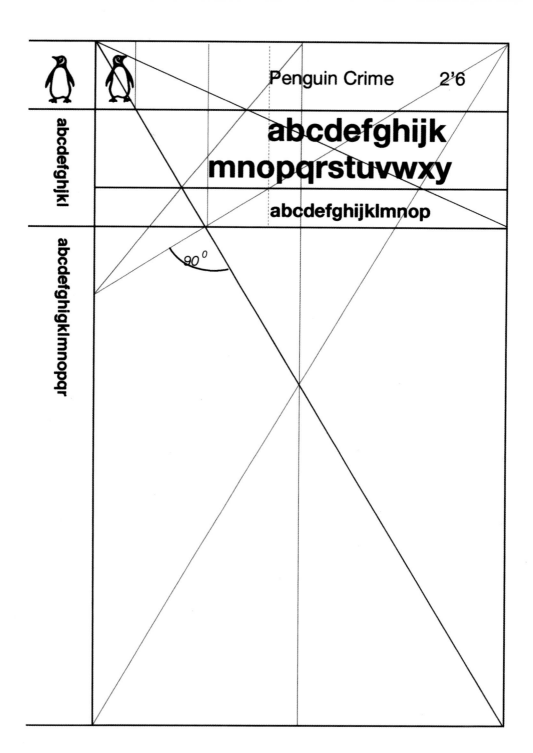

The Marber grid, 1961

In 1961 Germano Facetti, the Penguin Art Director, commissioned three designers to devise a new grid for the crime covers which would provide an area for illustration or graphic imagery but still retain a very clear and consistent typography. Romek Marber's solution was the one chosen, and he went on to illustrate around seventy titles in the series, with the remainder by other freelance designers commissioned by Facetti.

Marber retained the use of green to denote crime but lightened the shade considerably. A series of horizontal rules separated the publisher's name and symbol from the title and author's name. The typeface was Intertype Standard (a version of Berthold's Akzidenz Grotesk), which was closely associated with Swiss graphic design. Marber had been using it for a number of years and preferred its curves and differing weights to those of Helvetica, which was just starting to be used in Britain at that time. Titles in the crime series featured a more relaxed use of capitalization in the titles than other series, or indeed than standard British or American practice usually allowed.

The imagery used in the area below was often suggestive rather than literal, but even so, there was some adverse feedback about the 'darkness' of some of the images. They featured careful use of reversing-out and overprinting to make a virtue of the two-colour printing generally used. On a small number of titles a third colour – usually red – was used.

Recognizing the ability of the Marber grid to provide series unity and space for illustration, Germano Facetti also used it as the basis for both fiction and Pelican titles.

Its use for fiction was successful only when strong images were commissioned (pp. 106–7), and far less so when illustrations from the previous decade's 'vertical grid' were re-used.

For Pelican titles (pp. 108–11) Facetti commissioned designers rather than conventional illustrators. Several of them had received their first Penguin commissions during John Curtis's time in charge of covers, when photography and other approaches first began to feature regularly on covers. The graphic quality of these illustrations was every bit as good as those of the crime series and further validated the strength of Marber's original design.

Later in the 1960s strict observance of the grid was no longer thought necessary, but because covers were commissioned with care and were of a high standard with a consistent typographic feel, the series look was maintained (pp. 110–11). This policy would be continued through the next decade under the art direction of David Pelham (pp. 156–7 and 168–75).

OPPOSITE: The Marber grid, 1961.

Dreadful Summit, 1964.
Cover design by Germano Facetti.

The Case of the Half-Wakened Wife, 1963. Cover design by Romek Marber.

Boiled Alive, 1961.
Cover design by Romek Marber

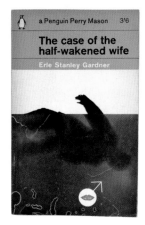

The D. A. Breaks a Seal, 1964. Cover design by Alan Aldridge.

Sweet Danger, 1963.
Cover design by Romek Marber.

Busman's Honeymoon, 1963.
Cover design by Romek Marber.

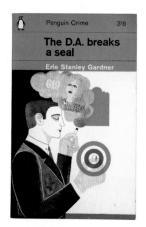

The Judas Window, 1962. Cover photograph by John Sewell.

Maigret Travels South, 1963.
Cover design by Geoffrey Martin.

The Case of the Caretaker's Cat, 1962. Cover design by Romek Marber.

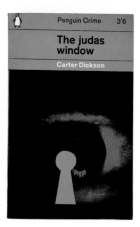

Penguin by Design

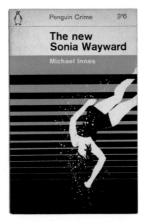

The Case of the Dangerous Dowager, 1962. Cover design by Romek Marber.

No Love Lost, 1961. Cover design by John Sewell.

The New Sonia Wayward, 1964. Cover drawing by Sydney King.

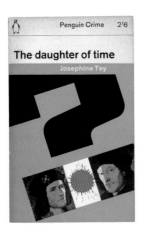

The Daughter of Time, 1961. Cover design by Romek Marber.

Lost Moorings, 1962. Cover design by Romek Marber.

The Night of Wenceslas, 1964. Cover photographs by Jean-Luc Blanc.

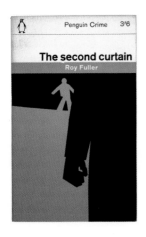

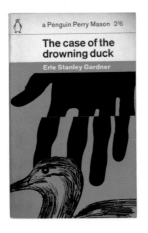

The Second Curtain, 1962. Cover design by Romek Marber.

The Case of the Drowning Duck, 1963. Cover design by George Daulby.

Your Money and Your Life, 1962. Cover design by George Mayhew.

The Widower, 1965.
Cover design by Leif Anisdahl.

The End of the Affair, 1962.
Cover drawing by Paul Hogarth.

The Bridge of San Luis Rey, 1963.
Cover design by Ursula Noerbel.

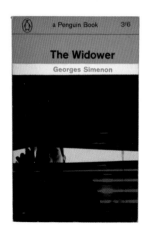  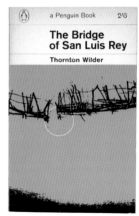

Rabbit, Run, 1964.
Cover drawing by Milton Glaser.

The Tunnel of Love, 1964.
Cover design by Alan Aldridge.

Striptease, 1963. Cover
drawing by Romek Marber.

 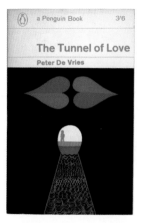 

A Gun for Sale, 1963.
Cover drawing by Paul Hogarth.

Nineteen Eighty-Four, 1962.
Cover design by Germano Facetti.

Lord Jim, 1965.
[The cover shows Peter O'Toole in
Richard Brooks' film *Lord Jim*.]

  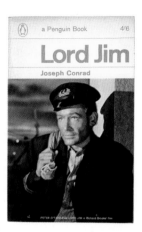

Penguin by Design

 a Penguin Book   5/-

Chosen
Words

Ivor Brown

The Stagnant Society, 1964.
Cover design by Germano Facetti.

Sex in Society, 1964.
Cover design by Jock Kinneir.

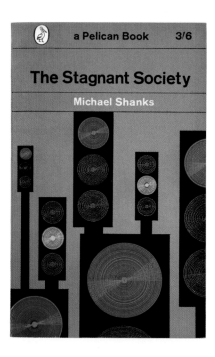

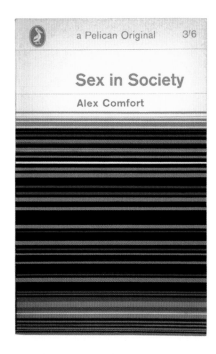

The Gothic Revival, 1964. Cover
photograph by Herbert Spencer.

Guide to the British Economy,
1965. Cover design by
Willock/Haynes/Aldridge.

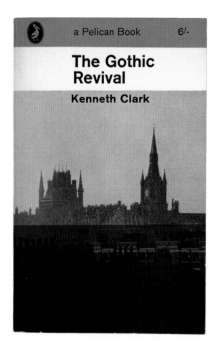

Penguin by Design

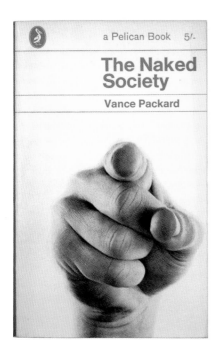

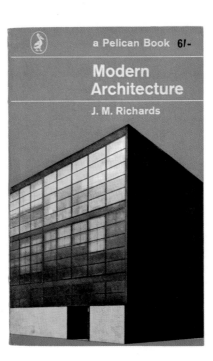

The Naked Society, 1964.
Cover design by Derek Birdsall.

Modern Architecture, 1963.
The illustration on the cover is
of a building forming part of the
Illinois Institute of Technology,
Chicago, by Mies van der Rohe.

Our Language, 1963.
Cover design by Romek Marber.

Silver, 1965. Cover design by
Bruce Robertson.

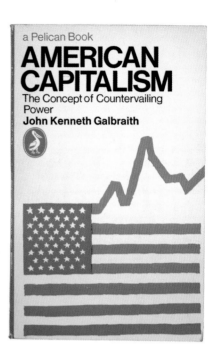

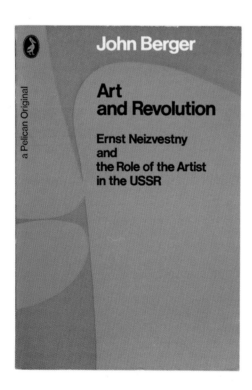

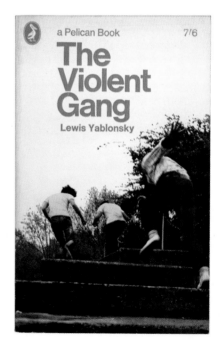

a Pelican Book

Britain in the Century of Total War
War, Peace and Social Change 1900–1967
Arthur Marwick

Britain in the Century of Total War, 1970. Cover painting by Barry Evans.

Specials in the sixties

Has Man a Future?, 1961.
[Cover design by Richard Hollis.]

The Specials enjoyed something of a renaissance in the 1960s, with titles reflecting the growing social awareness of society as it started to ask difficult questions of its leaders.

In the first half of the decade red dominated the designs so forcibly that it holds them together as a series despite all the other variations. Their only relationship to other titles overseen by Facetti is in the use of asymmetrically placed sans serif type – usually Helvetica or Grotesque 215/216. Covers were designed very quickly, in as little as a week, and made much use of stock photography and – like the Pelicans of the period – overprinting and a positive use of the white cover board. The urgency of a particular title was often stressed in its typography by highlighting a particular word in a different colour or size.

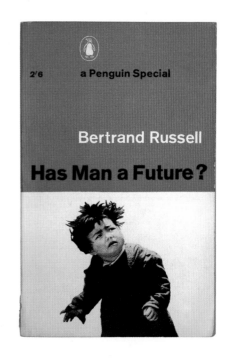

What's Wrong with the Unions?, 1961. Cover design by Bruce Robertson.

The covers of the second half of the 1960s (p. 115) seem less convincing as a series. There was a turn towards black as the dominant colour, and the covers exhibit a more regular typography (without size or colour changes within a title, for instance). The use of images tended also to be simpler, with untreated stock photography or a simple graphic 'idea' expressed in a reductive manner.

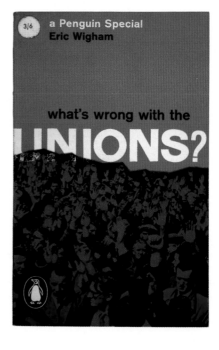

Penguin by Design

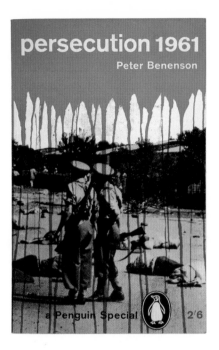

Persecution 1961, 1961. Cover design by Germano Facetti.

The A6 Murder, 1963. Cover design by Romek Marber.

Common Sense about Smoking, 1963. Cover design by Bruce Robertson.

Britain in the Sixties: Education for Tomorrow, 1962. Cover design by Richard Hollis.

The Police, 1964.
Cover design by Bruce Robertson.
Photograph by Keystone Press.

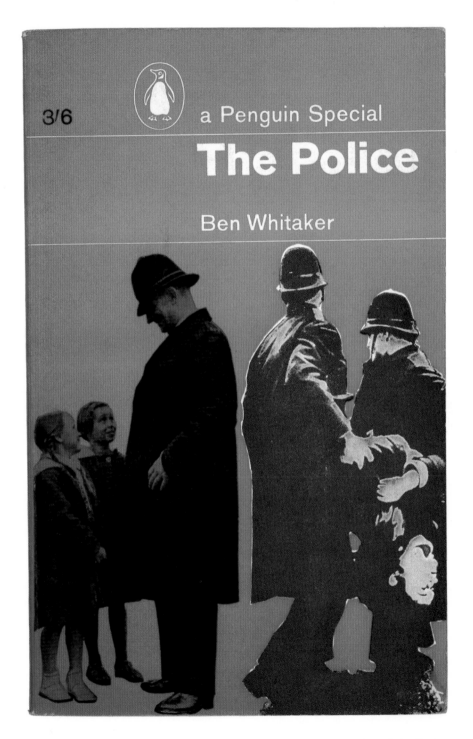

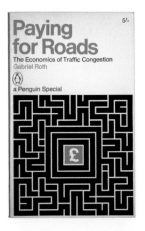

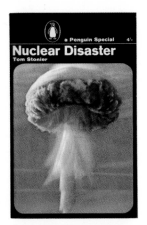

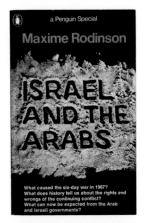

Paying for Roads, 1967.
Cover design by Brian Mayers.

Nuclear Disaster, 1964.

Israel and the Arabs, 1968.
Cover design by Stuart Flanagan.

After the Common Market,
1968. Cover design by Robert
Hollingsworth.

Drugs, 1968. Cover design by
Henning Boehlke.

*Is There Any Choice? Britain
Must Join Europe*, 1966.

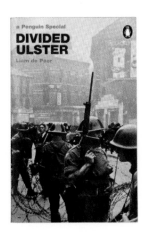

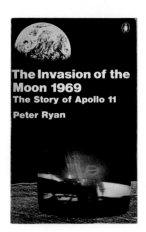

Divided Ulster, 1970. Cover
photograph by Camera Press.

The Invasion of the Moon 1969,
1969. Cover photo courtesy of
NASA.

*Demonstrations and
Communication: A Case Study*,
1970. The cover, designed by
Ralph Steadman, incorporates a
model of the American Embassy
by Shirt Sleeve Studios (Daily
Telegraph Colour Library).

'Books for egg-heads': Peregrines, 1962

The Rebel, 1969. Cover design by Graham Bishop.

Peregrines were introduced in 1962 as a series of unashamedly academic titles produced in B format to higher standards – heavier paper and better covers – than either Penguins or Pelicans. The Peregrine logo was designed by Hans Schleger (1898–1976) and on the front was positioned among a series of vertical stripes extending down from the top edge.

When these stripes were integrated into the design below by colour (*The Rebel* and *The Waning of the Middle Ages*) they are very distinctive, but when the two elements were treated separately (*The Rise of the Novel*) they are less satisfactory. Later designs in the series, such as *Some Shakespearean Themes and An Approach to Hamlet*, abandoned the stripes and employed a more predictable arrangement of type, logo and image.

OPPOSITE: *The Rise of the Novel*, 1966. Cover design by Bruce Robertson.

The Waning of the Middle Ages, 1968.

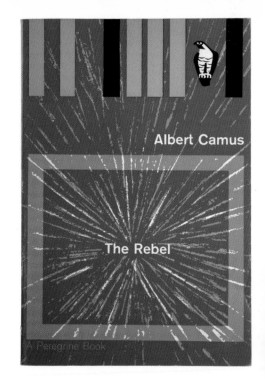

Cross Currents in English Literature of the Seventeenth Century, 1966. Cover design by Bruce Robertson.

OPPOSITE: *The Englishness of English Art*, 1964. Cover design by Herbert Spencer.

Some Shakespearean Themes and An Approach to Hamlet, 1966. Cover design by John Sewell.

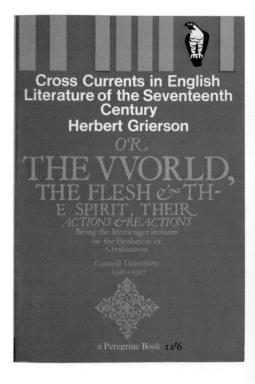

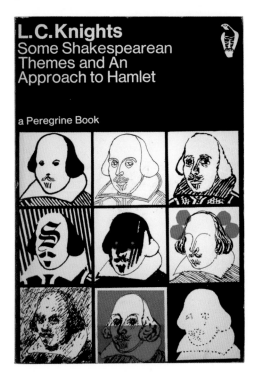

Penguin Modern Poets, 1962

Romek Marber's grid introduced a way of integrating text and image and retained the publisher's identity. It also brought about a return to a fixed style of typography that denied designers the possibilities of the typographic playfulness that John Curtis had encouraged a few years previously. This consistency, and the use of (largely) post-war sans serif types, was applied by Facetti across all the other series designs.

The aim of *Penguin Modern Poets*, as explained on the back cover, was '… to introduce contemporary poetry to a general reader by publishing some thirty poems by each of three modern poets in a single volume. In each case the selection is made to illustrate the poet's characteristics in style and form'.

A simple typographic style runs throughout the series, with condensed weights of the Univers typeface, capitals for the series title and upper and lower case for the authors' names. The exact position of this information was allowed to vary to accommodate the image.

The first seven titles feature stark, closely cropped black and white photographs or photograms, but colour was introduced with Volume 8, ushering in a slightly different use of photography (pp. 120–21).

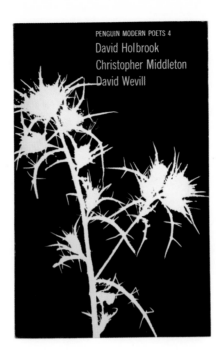

Penguin Modern Poets, Volume 3, 1970. Cover design by Peter Barrett.

Penguin Modern Poets, Volume 4, 1970. Cover design by Peter Barrett.

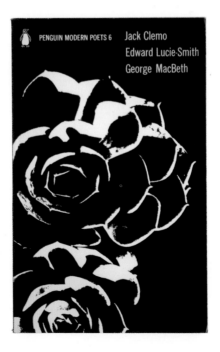

Penguin Modern Poets, Volume 5, 1969. Cover by Roger Mayne.

Penguin Modern Poets, Volume 6, 1970. Cover based on a photograph by Roger Mayne.

Penguin Modern Poets, Volume 7, 1965.

Penguin Modern Poets, Volume 8, 1968. Cover design by Alan Spain.

Penguin Modern Poets, Volume 9, 1971. Cover design by Alan Spain.

Penguin Modern Poets, Volume 10, 1967. Cover design by Alan Spain.

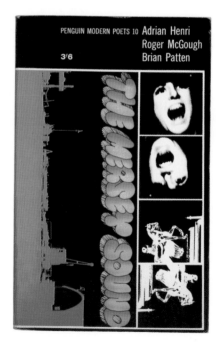

Penguin by Design

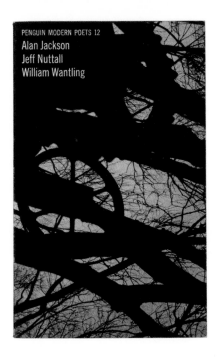

Penguin Modern Poets, Volume 12, 1968. Cover design by Alan Spain.

Penguin Modern Poets, Volume 13, 1969. Cover design by Alan Spain using a mineral specimen from Fisher, Overstone, Northampton.

Penguin Modern Poets, Volume 17, 1969. Cover photograph by Alan Spain.

Penguin Modern Poets, Volume 20, 1972. Cover design by Alan Spain.

Plays, 1964

Three Plays for Puritans, 1958.
[Cover design by John Miles.]

Penguin Plays were launched with the
publication of twelve of George Bernard
Shaw's stage works. Their initial design,
suggestive of a stage curtain, was by John
Miles (later to form a design partnership
with Colin Banks), but their best-known
cover design is that by Denise York,
introduced in 1964. This featured the
series title in lettering which mimics a
set of theatrical lights. Consistent typography for the playwrights and the play
titles is offset by a varied palette of
colours. Each cover used two – occasionally three – colours in addition to black,
but a careful use of overprinting created
the impression of more.

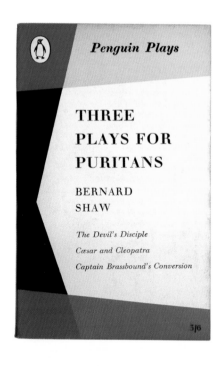

Plays Pleasant (back and front
cover), 1968. Cover design by
Denise York.

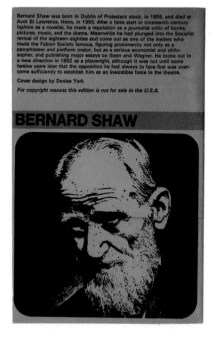

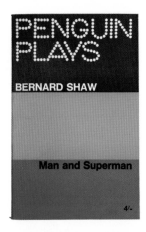

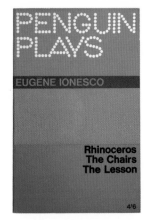

Three European Plays, 1965.
Cover design by Denise York.

Man and Superman, 1965.
Cover design by Denise York.

Rhinoceros and Other Plays,
1967. Cover design by
Denise York.

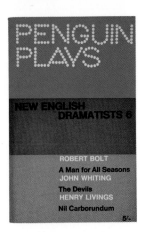

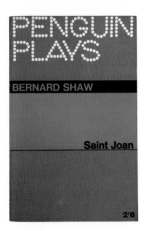

Parables for the Theatre, 1966.
Cover design by Denise York.

New English Dramatists,
Volume 6, 1966. Cover design
by Denise York.

Saint Joan, 1967.
Cover design by Denise York.

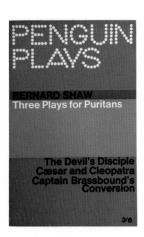

Plays (Oscar Wilde), 1964.
Cover design by Denise York.

Three Plays for Puritans, 1965.

Traverse Plays, 1966.

Classics, 1963

The Civil War, 1967.
The cover shows a Roman coin in the Bibliothèque Nationale, Paris (Snark International).

Having introduced the Marber grid for crime, fiction and Pelicans, Facetti turned his attention to unifying the appearance of the whole Penguin list. The Classics had used the same cover design since 1947 (p. 65), which, although well detailed, was not in keeping with the new look that was emerging. Facetti later described his approach to the redesign:

In designing for the Classics, it was assumed that the majority of the great works of literature have inspired works of art, or that works of art have been created with a bearing to literature. Besides the obvious 'desirability factors', the provision of a visual frame of reference to the work of literature can be considered an additional service to the reader who is without immediate access to art galleries or museums.

(Facetti, p. 24)

Presented soberly with black covers and spines, the new design featured photographic front covers, many of which were sourced from Snark, the Parisian agency Facetti had helped set up a few years previously. Depending on the nature of the image it could be used as a cut-out on a black background or extend over the whole front cover. The typeface used was Helvetica, and the only concession to classicism was the fact that it was set centred.

King Harald's Saga, 1966.
The cover shows a detail from the Baldishol Tapestry from Baldishol Church, Hedmark, Norway (end of twelfth century), now in the Museum of Applied Art, Oslo.

Beowulf, 1963.
The cover shows a helmet from
the Sutton Hoo treasure in the
British Museum.

Tender is the Night, 1963.
Cover illustration by John Sewell.

Tender is the Night, 1964.
Cover illustration by John Sewell.

Modern Classics

Modern Classics – a grouping of twentieth-century literature in new covers – was a series whose appearance took some time to settle down. When they first appeared it was to a design by Hans Schmoller with input from John Curtis and using Eric Gill's Joanna typeface.

When Facetti started using the Marber grid for crime, fiction and Pelicans (pp. 104–9) he also tried it out on some titles in Modern Classics but with the continued use of Joanna, at Schmoller's insistence.

Facetti described Joanna as 'scarcely apt for incisive display' (Facetti, p. 24) and it was some time before he got his way and introduced Helvetica to the series. A revised arrangement for the typography was introduced later in which the horizontal rule dividing author and title matches the height of the Classics 'grid' rather than the divisions of the Marber grid. Illustrations chosen for these covers, as in the main Classics series, tended to be contemporary with the period of each title's original publication.

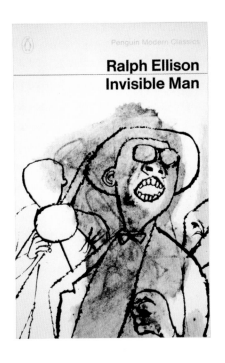

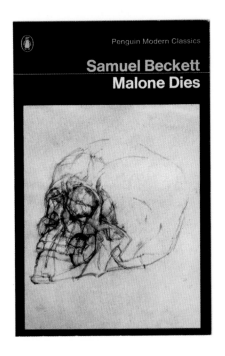

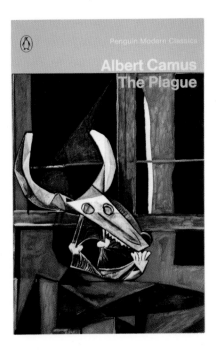

Invisible Man, 1968.
The cover shows a detail from one of a series of drawings by Ben Shahn commissioned for the film 'Ambassador Satchmo', reproduced by permission of the artist.

All About H. Hatterr, 1972.
The cover, designed by Germano Facetti, shows a detail from 'Two Saints in a Landscape' by F. N. Souza, in the Tate Gallery (photo John Webb).

Malone Dies, 1977.
The cover shows 'Skull 1923' by Alberto Giacometti by kind permission of Sir Robert Sainsbury (photo Rodney Todd-White).

The Plague, 1980.
The cover shows a detail from 'Nature morte au crâne de bœuf' by Pablo Picasso, Kunstsammlung, Düsseldorf.

Poetry restyled, 1963

Schmoller's popular 1954 poetry design was reworked in 1963. A smaller panel for the title was used to allow a greater area of the pattern to be appreciated. And what patterns! Far livelier than before, the juxtaposition of the two elements – the formal typography and the playful imagery – make this a much more interesting set of covers. Many of the designs were by Stephen Russ, some of whose artwork survives in the Penguin Archive at Bristol University.

Experimental layout and final cover for *The Penguin Book of Religious Verse*, 1963. Cover pattern by Stephen Russ.

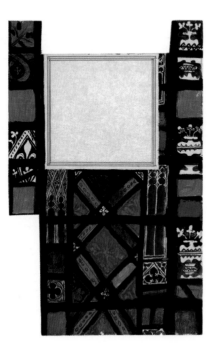

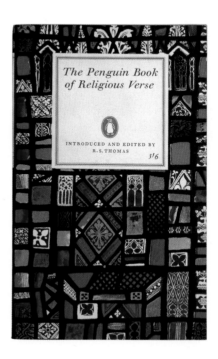

The Penguin Book of Religious Verse

INTRODUCED AND EDITED BY
R. S. THOMAS

3/6

Penguin by Design

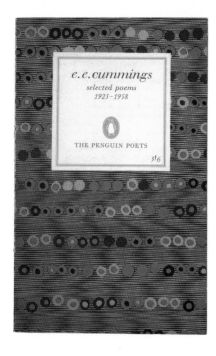

Experimental layout and final cover for *e. e. cummings*, 1963. [Cover pattern by Stephen Russ.]

Experimental layout and final cover for *Pushkin*, 1964. [Cover pattern by Stephen Russ.]

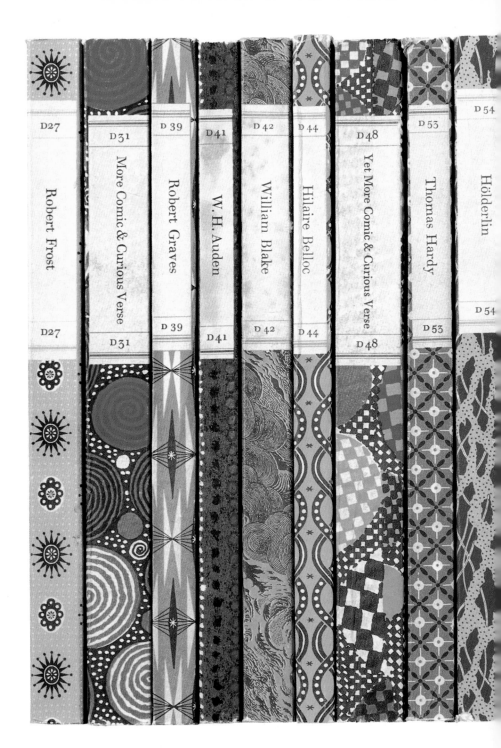

D27

Robert Frost

D27

D31

More Comic & Curious Verse

D31

D 39

Robert Graves

D 39

D41

W. H. Auden

D41

D 42

William Blake

D 42

D 44

Hilaire Belloc

D 44

D 48

Yet More Comic & Curious Verse

D 48

D 53

Thomas Hardy

D 53

D 54

Hölderlin

D 54

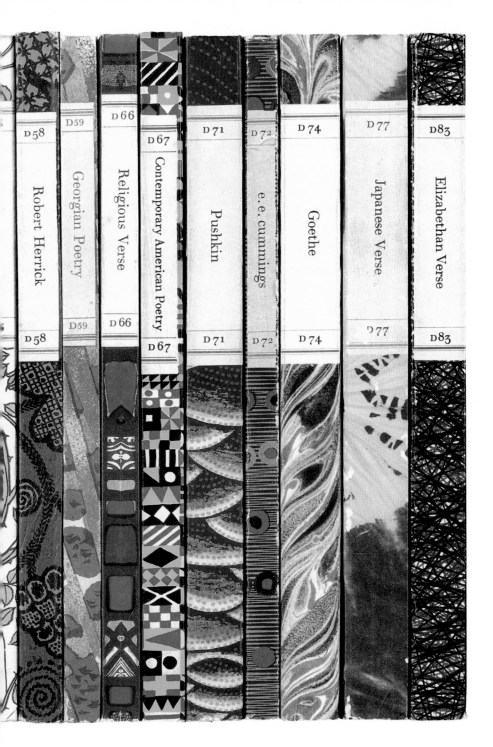

D58   D59   D66   D67   D71   D72   D74   D77   D83

Robert Herrick

Georgian Poetry

Religious Verse

Contemporary American Poetry

Pushkin

e. e. cummings

Goethe

Japanese Verse

Elizabethan Verse

Covers as posters:
Alan Aldridge, 1965

The Graduate, 1970.
The illustration on the cover
shows a scene from the Mike
Nichols–Lawrence Turman
production of *The Graduate*.

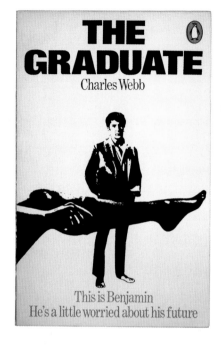

Tony Godwin had always known that
to compete with the likes of Pan and
Corgi Penguin couldn't rely on its reputation or the good taste of its cover
designs. It needed to ensure that its
books were given face-forward display
in bookshops, and to that end it needed
to make them particularly eye-catching.

Godwin appointed Alan Aldridge as
Fiction Art Director in 1965. Aldridge
was much younger than Facetti and
Schmoller; he had a sense of fun and a
desire to make his mark. He immediately brought change to the covers,
making sure that each was about the
title rather than about Penguin.

For standard fiction, there was no
unity, just a variety of cover styles using
photography, illustration or typography
as appropriate to attract the buyer's eye.
There was no consistency in the relationship between author name and title:
whichever was considered the most significant from a marketing point of view
was made dominant.

To help retain some sense of company identity the logo was enlarged considerably and its oval became a space
to add the colour that denoted fiction,
crime or science fiction. For crime titles,
the Marber grid was adapted and then
abandoned in favour of a totally free
style, and the older suggestive imagery
gave way to more obvious or explicit
versions (pp. 136–7).

Science fiction as a new sub-series
was given a more regular appearance,
with black covers, purple logos and
Aldridge's own highly worked fantasy
illustrations (pp. 138–9).

The Penguin John Lennon,
1966. Cover design by Aldridge.
Cover photograph by Duffy.

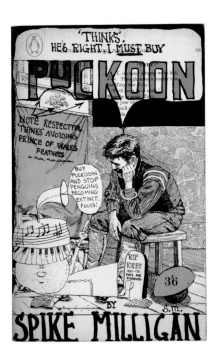

Funeral in Berlin, 1966. Cover design by Raymond Hawkey.

Puckoon, 1965.
Cover design by Spike Milligan.

Doctor in Clover, 1966. Elizabeth Ercy and Leslie Phillips as they appear in *Doctor in Clover* (A Betty E. Box–Ralph Thomas Production).

The Fall, 1966.

She Came to Stay, 1966. Cover
illustration by Giannetto
Coppola.

Girls in Their Married Bliss,
1967. Cover by Alan Aldridge.

Hurry On Down, 1966. Cover
illustration by Michael Foreman.

The Progress of Julius, 1967.
Cover illustration by
Renato Fratini.

Penguin by Design

Island, 1966.
Cover by Ross Cramer.

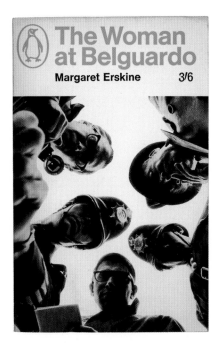

The Woman at Belguardo, 1966. Cover photograph by Dennis Rolfe.

Maigret's Special Murder, 1966. Cover design by Karl Ferris.

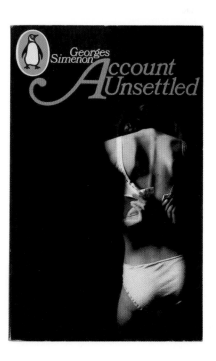

The Lady in the Lake, 1966. Cover photograph by Bob Brooks.

Account Unsettled, 1966. Cover photograph by Michael Busselle.

Destination: Void, 1967.
Cover design by Alan Aldridge.

The Wind from Nowhere, 1967.
Cover design by Alan Aldridge.

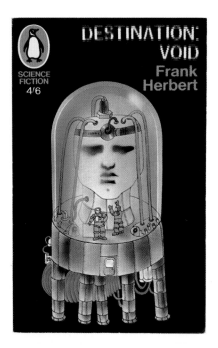

Tiger! Tiger!, 1967.
Cover by Alan Aldridge.

The Joyous Invasions, 1967.
Cover by Alan Aldridge.

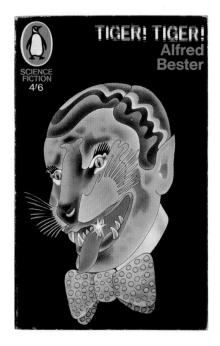

Penguin by Design

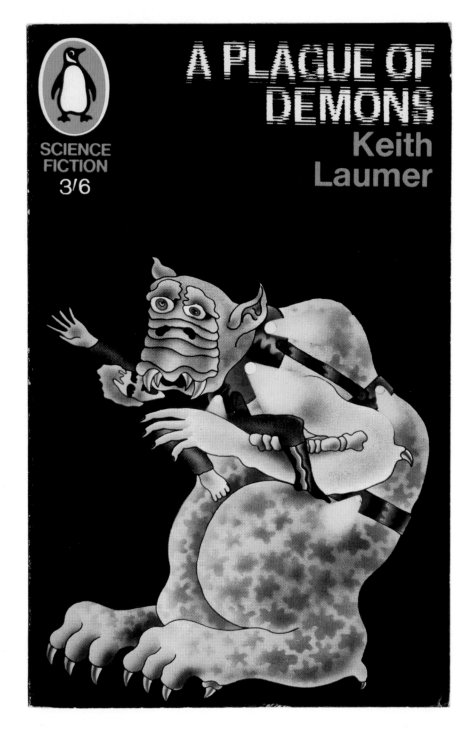

A *Plague of Demons*, 1967.
Cover design by Alan Aldridge.

Siné, *Massacre*, 1966

Having already published several collections of cartoons, Tony Godwin decided to publish the work of the French satirist Siné. The book contained an introduction by Malcolm Muggeridge which attempted to describe Siné and his work:

Afflicted as the imaginative necessarily are, with a heightened sense of the appalling disparity between human aspiration and human performance, Siné chooses to find relief in an irony which at one extreme shades into fantasy, at the other into disgust. (p. 6)

Nearly forty years later the work still has the power to shock. In 1966 many were outraged.

Upon publication many booksellers were disgusted by the book's contents and complained directly to Allen Lane, who they broadly regarded as having saved them from the worst excesses of cover vulgarity. *Private Eye* described the cartoons as 'grotesque' and reported:

Penguin (like the BBC) is so incompetently run that those in authority did not realize the nature of this work until it was too late. Now a full-scale boardroom rumpus has developed and resignations may follow. (9 December 1966)

At meetings most of the directors and editors at Penguin were against withdrawing the book, but soon afterwards, and despite this majority view, Allen Lane removed the entire unsold stock from the warehouse and took them to his home nearby. Whether they were burnt or buried is unclear. The title was subsequently listed as 'out of print'.

Post-Godwin panic, 1967–8

After Tony Godwin's departure Alan Aldridge's position as Art Director became increasingly difficult, and he left later that year. It was nearly another year before a replacement was appointed, and in the interim the line 'A PENGUIN BOOK', set in 36-point Optima, appeared across the top of every fiction cover, rarely with any sensitivity.

Since the 1950s J. D. Salinger had specific clauses in his contracts concerning the appearance of his books denying Penguin the right to include imagery or reviews on the covers. The carefully designed minimal cover of *Franny and Zooey* was fully appreciated only after the subsequent removal of the 'panic top'.

Alan Aldridge was asked by Allen Lane to commission Romek Marber to illustrate the Angus Wilson titles (his last for the company until 2005). Of his six covers only the first was printed as he had designed it; the others all had the 'panic top' added without him being informed. As with Salinger, the offending words were later removed, allowing Marber's original design to be seen as intended.

Edna O'Brien's books had featured 'blurb' prominently on their covers since the appearance of *Girls in Their Married Bliss* in 1967 (p. 134) with its distinctive hand-lettering. This idea was carried on with typography for her other books, but during the year of the 'panic top' the careful balance between the typography and the image was lost.

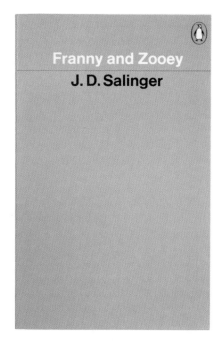

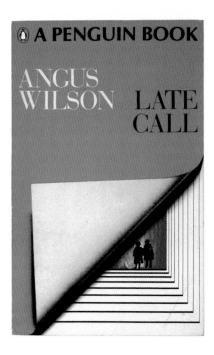

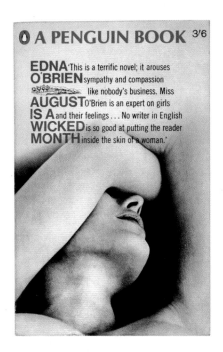

Late Call, 1968.
Cover design by Romek Marber.

August is a Wicked Month,
1967. Cover photograph from
'Mirror of Venus', a love story in
photographs by Wingate Paine,
words by Françoise Sagan and
Federico Fellini.

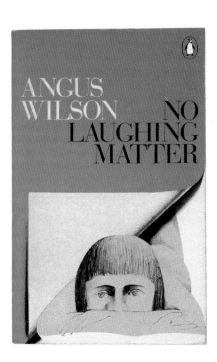

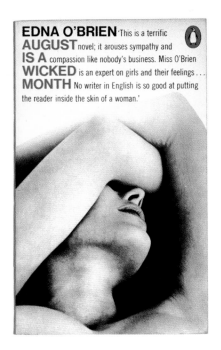

No Laughing Matter, 1969.
Cover design by Romek Marber.

August is a Wicked Month, 1969.
[Credit as above.]

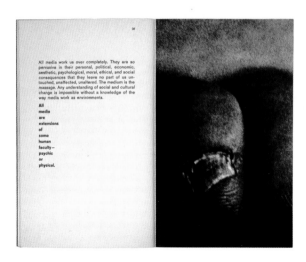
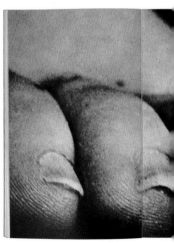

The Medium is the Massage, 1967. Cover photograph by Tony Rollo for *Newsweek*.

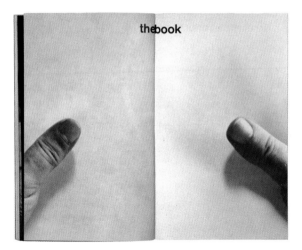

Integrated text and image:
The Medium is the Massage, 1967

'*… the title was a mistake. When the book came back from the typesetter, it had on the cover "Massage" as it still does. The title should have read* The Medium is the Message *but the typesetter had made an error. When Marshall McLuhan saw the typo he exclaimed, "Leave it alone! It's great, and right on target!" Now there are four possible readings for the last word of the title, all of them accurate: "Message" and "Mess Age", "Massage" and "Mass Age".'* (Eric McLuhan)

A popular reworking of McLuhan's writing – especially *The Gutenberg Galaxy* (1962) and *Understanding Media* (1964) – this was a collaborative project between

Penguin by Design

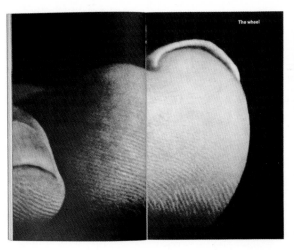

The wheel

...is an extension of the foot

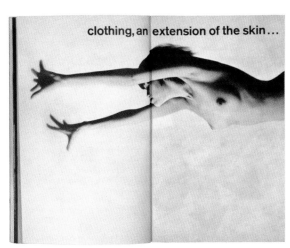
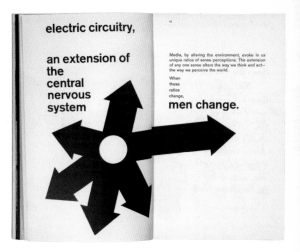

clothing, an extension of the skin...

electric circuitry,

an extension of
the
central
nervous
system

Media, by altering the environment, evoke in us
unique ratios of sense perceptions. The extension
of any one sense alters the way we think and act—
the way we perceive the world.

When
these
ratios
change,

men change.

McLuhan and graphic designer Quentin Fiore, with Jerome Agel as coordinator.

In designing the book they ignored the traditional text/image relationship in order to convey McLuhan's aphorisms with an urgency and drama lacking in the larger works from which they are extracted. Conventional text setting is used, but rarely for a complete page before a fragmented sequence of words and images

take you swiftly on several pages to the next point. The pace within these sequences is driven by the use of filmic devices such as changes in scale and cropping.

Forty years after it was first published this book is still popular with graphic designers – both for its commentary on media, technology and society, and for its design.

Poetry, 1966

The Penguin Book of Spanish Verse, 1966. [Pattern by Hans Schmoller.]

By 1966 the exquisite typography of the poetry series was beginning to look anachronistic in a Penguin list where every other series – except fiction – used contemporary sans serif typefaces.

Facetti continued with the idea of patterned backgrounds and simply updated the typography.

A Book of English Poetry, 1968.

Robert Frost, 1966.
Cover design by Stephen Russ.

Penguin by Design

Heine

Selected Verse
With an introduction
and prose translation by
Peter Branscombe
The Penguin Poets

Heine, 1967. Cover design by
Henning Boehlke.

Facetti Handbooks

Facetti updated the appearance of the Penguin Handbook series by giving it the same sans serif look as other lists.

He was not as uniform in his treatment of the series as he was elsewhere, however. Because Handbooks covered such a wide range of subjects, some titles naturally made sub-series and were given their own particular design to increase bookshop impact. The '*Improve Your ...*' sport titles are a good example of this.

For other interests (pp. 150–51) there was less of a series look, and the choice and style of imagery were intended to appeal specifically to the projected market for each title.

Improve Your Athletics, Volume 1, 1964. Cover design by Bruce Robertson. Photograph by Keystone Press.

Improve Your Athletics, Volume 2, 1964. Cover design by Bruce Robertson. Photograph by Toni Nett.

Improve Your Golf, 1966.
Cover design by Bruce Robertson.

Improve Your Tennis, 1966.
Cover design by Bruce Robertson.

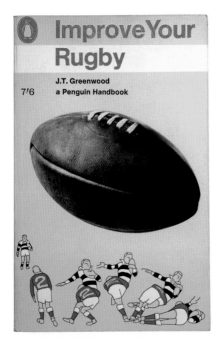

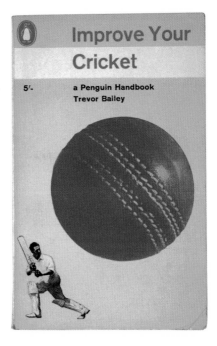

Improve Your Rugby, 1967.
Cover design by Bruce Robertson.

Improve Your Cricket, 1963.
Cover design by Bruce Robertson.

*The New Vegetable Grower's
Handbook*, 1962. Cover design
by Bruce Robertson.

He and She, 1968.
Cover design by Bruce Robertson.
Photograph by Dietmar Kautzsch.

Design to Fit the Family, 1965.
Cover photographs by Ian
Yeomans of a room designed
by John Winter.

Sailing, 1966.
The cover shows an ocean racing
yacht (Picture-point photograph).

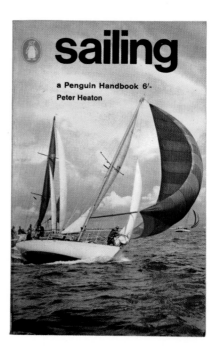

Penguin by Design

New Penguin Shakespeare, 1967

Since 1949 Penguin Shakespeare had
appeared in the dependable Tschichold
cover (pp. 60–61). Despite its impecc-
able detailing, the grace it once had
when printed by letterpress on uncoated
board was lost once covers began to be
printed by offset-litho and were gloss-
laminated. The other problem with the
design – as with the horizontal stripes of
the original Penguin main series – was
that one title looked much like another.

For the New Penguin Shakespeare
introduced from 1967 onwards Facetti
originally used a design similar to the
Classics series design but with a swelled
rule rather than a fine white line. While
this scheme was retained for the com-
mentaries, some of which featured
beautifully lit still-life photography of
books (pp. 154–5), it was used for only
the first seven plays.

An entirely new approach was then
begun with a stronger use of typography
that made a clear distinction between
the series name and the title of the play.
Facetti retained the white background
from the old design and commissioned
David Gentleman to provide an illustration for each play.

Gentleman produced a series of
woodcuts suggestive of medieval illustrations but with simple coloured areas
to give them variety. Each cover is
printed in black and up to four other
colours. (In the mid 1970s he used a
similar technique when designing the
murals for the Northern Line platforms
at the Charing Cross underground
station redevelopment.)

New Penguin Shakespeare

Henry IV, Part 1

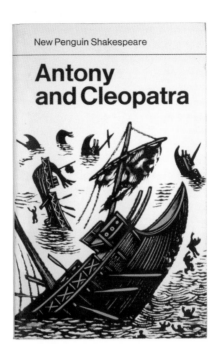

New Penguin Shakespeare

Antony and Cleopatra

Henry IV, Part 1, 1968. Cover design by David Gentleman.

Antony and Cleopatra, 1977. Cover design by David Gentleman.

New Penguin Shakespeare

King John

New Penguin Shakespeare

Macbeth

King John, 1974. Cover design by David Gentleman.

Macbeth, 1978. Cover design by David Gentleman.

Shakespeare's Comedies, 1967.
Cover photo by Alan Spain and
Nelson Christmas.

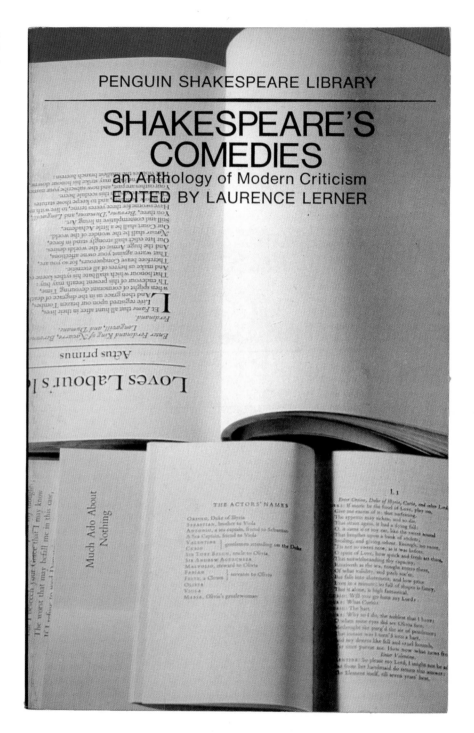

Penguin by Design

Shakespeare and the Idea of the Play, 1967. Cover photo by Alan Spain and Nelson Christmas.

David Pelham and science fiction, 1968

The Squares of the City, 1969.
Cover design by Franco Grignani.

Following Alan Aldridge's departure and
a year without a Fiction Art Director,
David Pelham was appointed in 1968.
He tried to combine the freedom of the
Aldridge front cover with consistent
spine and back covers which held the
publisher's identity. For the front cover
he defined set corner positions for the
logo but left the position of everything
else down to the individual designer
or illustrator. His early designs for the
science fiction series continue the strong
colours introduced by Aldridge but
are here used with images derived from
photography.

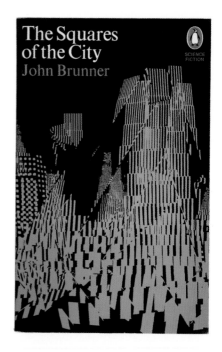

Time Out of Joint, 1969.
Cover design by Franco Grignani.

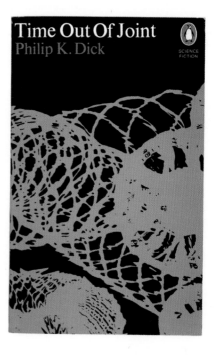

Penguin by Design

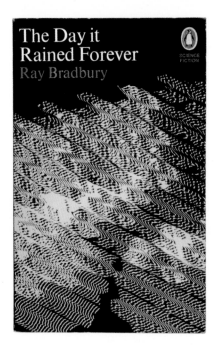

The Day It Rained Forever, 1969.
Cover design by Franco Grignani.

Davy, 1969.
Cover design by Franco Grignani.

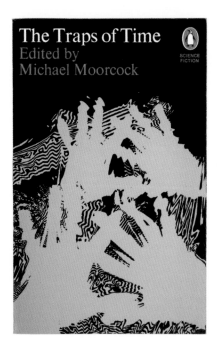

The Traps of Time, 1970.
Cover design by Franco Grignani.

Rork!, 1969.
Cover design by Franco Grignani.

Penguin no. 3000, 1969

OPPOSITE: *Ulysses*, 1969.

Just as with anniversaries, Penguin was conscious of marking significant numbers in its list with carefully chosen titles. In 1969, International Standard Book Numbers (ISBNs) were to be embraced by Penguin. These would detract from their own series numbering, but before that took place no. 3000 was reached and by chance it coincided with the fiftieth anniversary of Allen Lane's entry into publishing. It was decided to celebrate with the first paperback publication of James Joyce's *Ulysses*.

In 1934, Allen Lane had bought the rights to publish *Ulysses* in its first British edition for The Bodley Head. The other directors of the company disagreed and the brothers bore the financial risk themselves. It appeared in 1936.

To emphasize its importance, and unusually for that period, *Ulysses* was printed in the larger B format. Germano Facetti wanted the cover to appear in the now-standardized Modern Classics series design (p. 127), but Hans Schmoller presented the design shown here and used his position to push it through. Purely typographic, and deceptively simple, it features Jan Van Krimpen's typeface Spectrum (1952) but with redrawn capitals. Although it doesn't relate to the rest of the Modern Classics – or indeed to anything else art-directed by Facetti – it is a very striking cover and one of the most memorable from that period.

James
Joyce
Ulysses

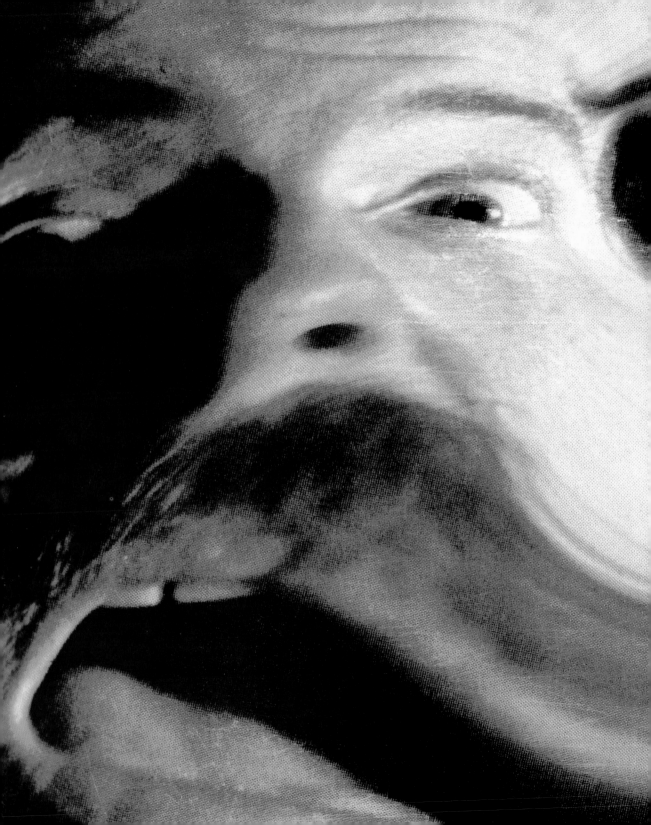

Detail taken from *The John Franklin Bardin Omnibus*, 1976 (p. 179). Photograph by Paul Wakefield.

IV. Life after Lane, 1970–95

IV. Life after Lane, 1970–95

1. Quoted in Graham, p. 58.

Derek Birdsall

While Allen Lane's death and the change of ownership clearly represented the end of an era for Penguin, for the publishing business generally the dawn of the 1970s was a time of changing priorities, with the emphasis shifting away from the intrinsic value of books themselves towards the potential profit to be made out of marketing them successfully. The financial uncertainties of the early 1970s only made this more inevitable, and the various mergers and acquisitions that have occurred since – beginning with Pearson's merger of Penguin and the American hardback imprint Viking in 1975 – have reinforced the profit-oriented nature of modern publishing.

At Penguin these changes did not affect the appearance of books for some time, because the senior designers, Facetti, Schmoller and Pelham, all retained their respective roles and many of the same freelance designers continued to provide covers.

The design of fiction, science fiction and crime books continued to be driven essentially by the needs of the individual titles, with appropriately coloured spines and the Penguin logo being the sole brand identifiers. Pelham later described what he wanted a cover to do:

There must be two triggers – an initial trigger which will attract the buyer to-wards the book from the other side of the shop; and then, when he gets to the book, a second trigger which is in some visual and/or literal way intriguing. Then, he actually reaches out and picks the book up. [1]

But away from fiction, continuity of the Penguin brand was assured by the look of established series such as the Classics and Modern Classics, which retained their fixed styles and provided some visual calm at the centre of the list. Penguin Education was given a new, more varied look when David Pelham commissioned Derek Birdsall's company Omnific to oversee the re-design of the complete series in 1971–2, but it retained its very strong brand identity, keeping its own descriptive logo drawn by Hans Schleger in 1967.

The first three senior executives of Penguin following the takeover – Christopher Dolley, Peter Calvocoressi and Jim Rose – had the unenviable task of steering the company through a time of great economic difficulty. In 1974 Calvocoressi cut the planned publication programme from 800 titles to 450 and closed the Education list. University-level titles remained in print, but with different covers accommodated in other series, while those aimed at levels below were dropped entirely.

There were also pressures within the book trade itself. Since the 1960s more hardback publishers had started paperback imprints of their own. This, and the increasing number of paperback publishers, created more competition and higher licence fees for paperback titles. Moreover, in the early 1970s several hardback publishers reclaimed the rights to a number of authors' works, including those of Hemingway, Huxley, Joyce and Murdoch.

2. Facetti, p. 77.

Peter Mayer

Changes in the Penguin design departments began with the departure of Germano Facetti. He left in 1972, though his contribution had been reduced to twenty-two hours a week for some time before that. He returned to Italy a year later, having brought to Penguin a stylish unity across the many disparate parts of the list and having fostered an intellectual approach to design and the use of photography. Writing of his work in 1969 he said:

Not all the covers shown here are thrilling from the point of view of design. It is much more important that Penguin has established a high standard throughout, rather than swinging from good to bad, cover to cover, as almost all other publishers do.[2]

In 1976, after twenty-seven years at Penguin, Hans Schmoller retired. Schmoller's talents lay principally inside the books, and since the late 1950s he had concentrated on that aspect of design and on the detailing of typography. He ensured that everyone adhered to his own very high standards. Since the founding of Penguin Books, Allen Lane had stressed the importance of good design and had always been prepared to pay for it. In Schmoller he was paid back for that investment many times over. Schmoller's role at Penguin was continued by Fred Price until 1979, and then by Jerry Cinamon until his retirement in 1986.

In 1978 a new Managing Director was appointed. Peter Mayer, who had previously been publisher at Avon Books and Pocket Books in the USA, was given the task of revitalizing the company. He recognized that Penguin had become a sleeping giant and set about changing the company's attitude towards marketing. Fiction titles began to appear in different formats, and heavy publicity was used to promote certain of them. Perhaps the biggest success of the period was M. M. Kaye's *The Far Pavilions*, with the TV adaptation exploited to generate maximum sales. While these activities undoubtedly helped the company's fortunes, their effect on the cover designs might best be described as 'varied'. By the early 1980s many Penguin books, with their insensitive combinations of type and image, looked like the cheapest in the bookshop.

3. Interview with Linda Lloyd Jones and Jeremy Aynsley, June 1984. Bristol Archive, DM1585/6 & 18.

Under Mayer's management the messages about identity were contradictory. The use of orange as a brand identifier on fiction was repeatedly questioned, lambasted and stoutly defended in turn. Such vacillation was fortunately offset by the consistent design styles applied to other series. That these smaller series carried and upheld the Penguin brand, while the fiction list concentrated on individual titles and market share, was of crucial importance after the difficult 1970s.

While many will argue that, from a design point of view, Mayer's era marks the all-time low in quality at Penguin, that opinion obscures the fact that, while the company made a loss of £242,000 in 1979, it made a £5·64 million profit only three years later. Mayer's view was that 10–15 per cent of the books would have to change radically in order to secure their market share and thus safeguard the remainder of Penguin's output, and the company's survival was more important than design ideals or standards.

David Pelham resigned as Art Director in 1979, having been frustrated for some time by the changes around him. Speaking a few years later about that time he said:

The art department ... became the whipping boys, because if a book didn't sell, if the editor had made a mistake, if the marketing people hadn't pulled their finger out, if they had pulled it out in the wrong direction, they could always say 'Sorry, it was the cover, it was never the book, it was never anything else.' So you got a lot of flak in spite of the fact that they had all in a democratic way sat around a table and said 'Yes, we'll go with that.'[3]

Pelham was succeeded by Cherriwyn Magill, previously at Penguin and then Macmillan. The Modern Classics were restyled by her, and she commissioned Ken Carroll and Mike Dempsey (later to form the design group Carroll, Dempsey and Thirkell with Nick Thirkell) to redesign Reference. The King Penguin name was resurrected in 1981, this time for a paperback list showcasing contemporary fiction, with a series style by Carroll and Dempsey designed to accommodate commissioned illustrations.

There is a certain politeness in much of the typography of the early 1980s covers, characterized by the use of serifed, often condensed, 'Modern' typefaces (pp. 212–13), perhaps as a reaction to the perceived visual poverty of modernism. There are references to various historical periods in the form of typographic details such as patterned borders or rules, but on the whole it is done with little depth of knowledge and none of the craft skills associated with classical setting. In part these covers represent visual trends of the time, but they are also the work of a generation of designers from an art school rather than a trade printing background, using typesetting houses who were often struggling with the demands of expensive new typesetting equipment and unsure how to apply the inherited skills of metal type to that new technology.

Another Mayer marketing strategy was an increased use of the larger B format, and much of the Design Department's time was spent converting existing artwork to the new size. Although the type itself was slightly enlarged, books adjusted in this way were easy to tell because of the unusually generous margins around the text area. There was considerable criticism at the time that this was nothing more than a cynical marketing ploy – the increase in retail price was greater than the increased production cost – and that Penguin was betraying its origins, which lay in providing good reading at the cheapest possible price.

At the same time, Mayer decided that the previous Penguin practice of re-typesetting every title bought from other publishers and styling it to conform with the Composition Rules could no longer be justified if that practice made publishing a title uneconomic. New titles could now simply be photographically reproduced ('offset'), with Penguin only needing to generate new preliminary pages (the title page, imprint page, and so on). While this undoubtedly made the publication of certain titles viable, it was at the expense of a consistent appearance and was a dilution of the high standards built up by the company since Tschichold's reforms in 1947.

There were changes in location also. In 1979 the Art Department and editors – at John Street, Holborn, since the 1960s – moved to larger premises on the New Kings Road, Chelsea, and in 1985 the addition of Michael Joseph and Hamish Hamilton to the Pearson portfolio – Frederick Warne having been acquired two years previously – meant that further relocation was necessary. The editorial and design teams now moved to Wrights Lane in Kensington.

In 1984 Magill left and Steve Kent took over. Among his first jobs was the redesign of the Classics series. For this, only its third significant design, he reverted to a serifed typeface – Sabon – and a 'panel' design similar to that favoured in the 1950s. The redesign was launched in August 1985, the company's fiftieth year.

Penguin celebrated that anniversary with an exhibition at the Royal Festival Hall in London, but for many older employees of the firm another link with the past disappeared with the death, soon afterwards, of Hans Schmoller. Schmoller's work was celebrated by Jerry Cinamon and others

4. This did not initially affect the design of text pages, which was still done in the time-honoured way of casting-off a manuscript (that is, calculating its length), and then marking it up with instructions for a trade typesetting house to follow.

in a special issue of the Monotype Corporation's journal *Monotype Recorder*, which appeared the following year.

The senior management of the company changed again during the late 1980s as Mayer became more involved in Penguin's American operations. Trevor Glover – previously Managing Director of Penguin Australia – returned in 1987 to become Managing Director, to be followed in 1996 by Anthony Forbes Watson.

In 1991, to the dismay of many, Pelicans were ended as a separate imprint. Created by Allen Lane in 1937 to provide the serious reader with authoritative books on a variety of subjects, it was felt that they had begun to be perceived by the public as too high-brow, and that therefore the Pelican livery was a barrier to sales. The fact that the Pelican name couldn't be used by Penguin in the US, where another publisher had an imprint of that name, only made it more inevitable that the Pelicans' time was up. As with the Education series titles before, books from the list continued to be published elsewhere, and several of the 'Pelican histories' have become 'Penguin histories'.

Changes in production occurred again in the early 1990s, as the Apple Macintosh was introduced to the art departments by Production Director Jonathan Yglesias. Used by designers soon after its appearance in the United States in 1984, it was the first personal computer system to offer page-layout programs, readily available fonts, and a 'graphic user interface' in one convenient package.4 Cover designers benefited from the immediacy of design programs such as QuarkXPress, Freehand and Illustrator, and image-manipulation software like PhotoShop. The ability to preview designs – with typography and imagery combined – on-screen made it possible to try out multiple solutions quickly, and, if necessary, for discussions to take place around a computer. The merging of creative and production roles was met with misgivings by some (reflecting concerns throughout the graphic design profession generally), but the positive aspects of the new ways of working made it possible for a greater dialogue to occur between editors, picture researchers and designers. This process continues today.

OPPOSITE: *The Far Pavilions*, 1979. Cover illustration by Dave Holmes and Peter Goodfellow.

OPPOSITE: When M. M. Kaye's *The Far Pavilions* was published by Penguin in 1979, it was given a jacket unlike the majority of fiction covers the company then produced. This was unashamedly a 'selling cover' and marked a new, more aggressive approach by the company to achieving sales and reversing the financial difficulties of the previous years.

Penguin by Design

M. M. KAYE
THE FAR PAVILIONS

**The great
bestseller!
A story of
love and war
as towering as
the Himalayas**

David Pelham's fiction non-grid

Words, 1983.
Cover design by Omnific.

David Pelham's approach to the fiction covers combined the freedom of Alan Aldridge with a far more consistent spine and back cover treatment to hold the publisher's identity. For the front cover he defined a set of positions for the logo but left the arrangement of everything else down to the individual designer or illustrator. If there is a unifying feature of his covers it is the quality of the typographic detailing and its integration with the other elements of the design.

As with Aldridge, the cover treatments responded to each title, and illustration, photography, design and typography were all used as he felt appropriate. His art direction also reflected an approach to the use of period style different from either Aldridge's or Facetti's. Aldridge had used styles such as art nouveau to attract attention rather than as historical signifiers, and Facetti introduced history only through the illustrative element. Pelham saw the need to attract attention but wanted covers which did that for a reason. He did not have Facetti's purist attitude to aesthetics, and when he felt it appropriate he commissioned covers which were unashamedly nostalgic. Perhaps the best examples of this were the covers for the Evelyn Waugh titles designed by Bentley/Farrell/Burnett (p. 172).

The practice of giving certain authors their own distinctive treatment, which was begun in the 1950s (p. 81), was continued under Pelham, and four very different expressions of that idea are shown on the following two spreads.

Yukiko, 1980.
Cover design by John Gorham.

A Clockwork Orange, 1985.
Cover design by David Pelham.

Penguin by Design

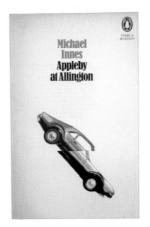

Danger UXB, 1981. Cover design by Neil Stuart. Cover illustration by Chermayeff & Geismar.

Two Views, 1971. Cover design by Roland Box.

Appleby at Allington, 1971. Cover design by Crosby/Fletcher/Forbes.

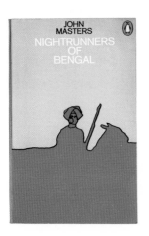

Nightrunners of Bengal, 1971. Cover design by Steve Dwoskin.

Kes, 1982. Line [i.e. not halftone] treatment on cover photograph by Enzo Ragazzini.

Save Me the Waltz, 1971. Cover design by Bentley/Farrell/Burnett.

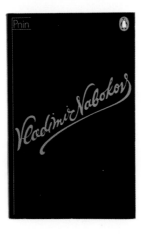

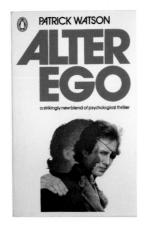

The Train Was On Time, 1979. Cover illustration by Candy Amsden.

Pnin, 1971. Cover design by John Gorham.

Alter Ego, 1979. Cover illustration by Danny Kleinman.

Bonjour Tristesse, 1976. Cover
photograph by Ian Hessenberg.

Those without Shadows, 1973.
Cover photograph by Steve
Campbell.

The Heart-Keeper, 1978. Cover
photograph by Steve Campbell.

A Certain Smile, 1969. Cover
photograph by Van Pariser.

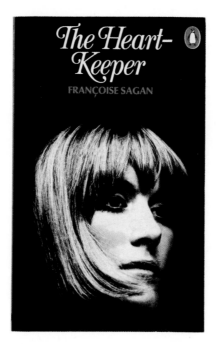 

Penguin by Design

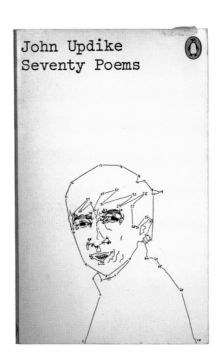

Rabbit, Run, 1970. Cover design by Derek Birdsall/ Michael Foreman.

Pigeon Feathers & Other Stories, 1978. Cover design by Derek Birdsall/Michael Foreman.

The Same Door, 1968. Cover design by Derek Birdsall/ Michael Foreman.

Seventy Poems, 1972. Cover design by Derek Birdsall/ Michael Foreman.

Black Mischief, 1988. Cover design by Bentley/Farrell/Burnett.

Put Out More Flags, 1987. Cover design by Bentley/Farrell/Burnett.

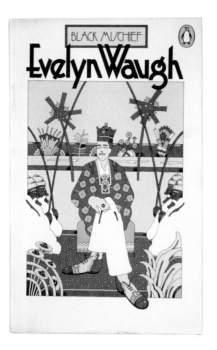 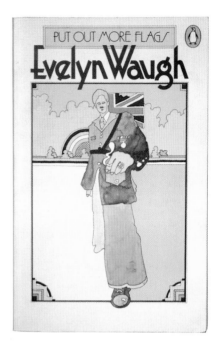

Helena, 1987. Cover design by Bentley/Farrell/Burnett.

Scoop, 1984. Cover design by Bentley/Farrell/Burnett.

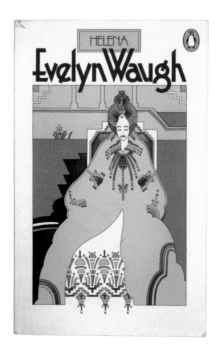 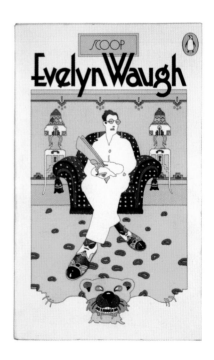

Penguin by Design

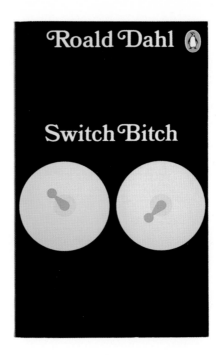

Someone Like You, 1982.
Cover design by Omnific.

Switch Bitch, 1982.
Cover design by David Pelham.

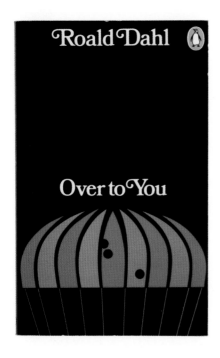

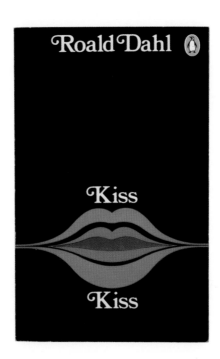

Over to You, 1973.
Cover design by Omnific.

Kiss Kiss, 1970.
Cover design by Omnific.

The End of the Affair, 1971.
Cover illustration by
Paul Hogarth.

The End of the Affair, 1973.
Cover design by Derek Birdsall.

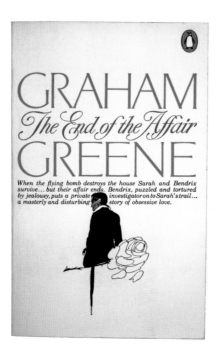

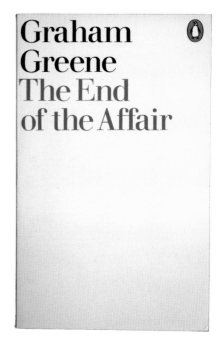

Our Man in Havana, 1968.
Cover illustration by
Paul Hogarth.

Our Man in Havana, 1973.
Cover design by Derek Birdsall.

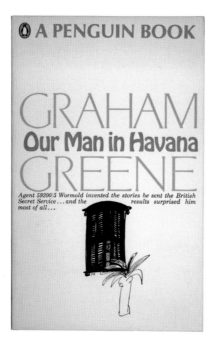

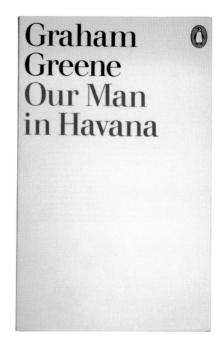

Penguin by Design

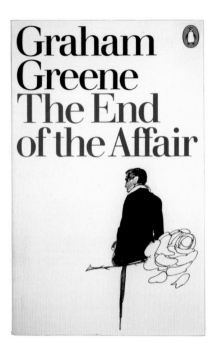

A failed experiment

One reason given for the curious lack of illustrations on a number of Graham Greene covers is that his approval had not been forthcoming. An alternative explanation is as follows.

Despite being happy with the Paul Hogarth illustrations used on his books, Graham Greene felt the books were selling well on the strength of his name alone, and he rang up Art Director David Pelham to discuss the possibility of purely typographic covers. Pelham felt this was wrong and asked Derek Birdsall to call Greene and persuade him otherwise. The phone conversation with Greene had the opposite effect, and Birdsall rang Pelham to say he felt Greene may have a point. Pelham then asked Birdsall to design the typographic covers for a couple of titles, which duly appeared in the bookshops. Sales fell dramatically. For the next reprint Paul Hogarth's paintings reappeared on the covers and, as if to compensate for what had happened, both image and type were enlarged considerably.

Shown here are the three sequential cover designs for two of the titles.

The End of the Affair, 1975.
Cover illustration by
Paul Hogarth.

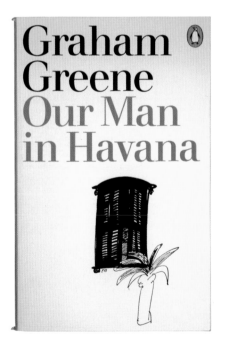

Our Man in Havana, 1975.
Cover illustration by
Paul Hogarth.

Ways of Seeing, 1972

The cover of this book is a conceit. It appears as though the text actually begins there on the cover – which was its makers' intention – but established practice prevails and it has a conventional title page and starts beyond. A co-publication with the BBC, both the cover and contents of *Ways of Seeing* were designed by Richard Hollis.

Containing seven essays, four of text and images, three of images only, *Ways of Seeing* was an unusual form of integrated book. Printed in black only, it is not a visual essay like *The Medium is the Massage* (pp. 144–5), which has a distinct film-like quality. In the word/image essays in *Ways of Seeing* the words are the prevailing voice, with images placed exactly where they are discussed. To reinforce the dominant aspect of the text it is set, not in the regular weight of a serif typeface, but in the bold weight of the sans serif Univers. Each paragraph is indicated by deep indents (about a quarter of a line long) that also mark one of the points from which images are aligned.

The book's design was particularly disliked by Hans Schmoller. 'Is this meant to be centred?' was written angrily across cover proofs returned to the designer, and when the printed book was placed on his desk he promptly hurled it down the corridor in disgust.

a Pelican Original

WAYS OF SEEING

Based on the BBC television series with

JOHN BERGER

Seeing comes before words. The child looks and recognizes before it can speak.

But there is also another sense in which seeing comes before words. It is seeing which establishes our place in the surrounding world; we explain that world with words, but words can never undo the fact that we are surrounded by it. The relation between what we see and what we know is never settled.

The door   The wind

The bird   The valise

The Surrealist painter Magritte commented on this always-present gap between words and seeing in a painting called The Key of Dreams.

The way we see things is affected by what we

WAYS OF SEEING

based on the BBC television series with

JOHN BERGER

British Broadcasting Corporation and Penguin Books

She is not naked as she is.
She is naked as the spectator sees her.

Often – as with the favourite subject of Susannah and the Elders – this is the actual theme of the picture. We join the Elders to spy on Susannah taking her bath. She looks back at us looking at her.

SUSANNAH AND THE ELDERS BY TINTORETTO

In another version of the subject by Tintoretto, Susannah is looking at herself in a mirror. Thus she joins the spectators of herself.

SUSANNAH AND THE ELDERS BY TINTORETTO 1518–1594

The mirror was often used as a symbol of the vanity of woman. The moralizing, however, was mostly hypocritical.

VANITY BY MEMLING 1435–1494

You painted a naked woman because you enjoyed looking at her, you put a mirror in her hand and you called the painting *Vanity*, thus morally condemning the woman whose nakedness you had depicted for your own pleasure.

The real function of the mirror was otherwise. It was to make the woman connive in treating herself as, first and foremost, a sight.

The Judgement of Paris was another theme with the same inwritten idea of a man or men looking at naked women.

THE JUDGEMENT OF PARIS BY CRANACH 1472–1553

The Dick, 1973. Cover
photograph by Dennis Rolfe.

Final Curtain, 1978. Cover
design by Robert Hollingsworth,
photograph by Peter Barbieri.

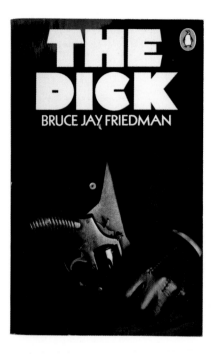

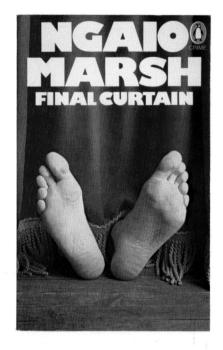

The Night of Wenceslas, 1977.
Cover photograph by
Robert Golden.

Inside Information, 1978. Cover
photograph by Robert Golden.

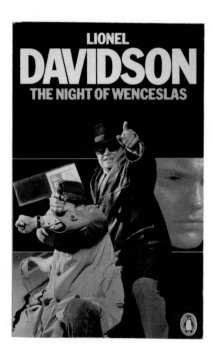

Penguin by Design

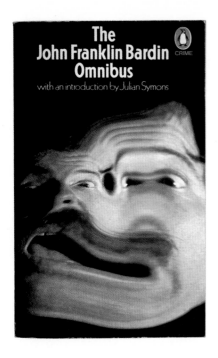

Crime crimes

With the first illustrative crime covers in the early 1960s it had been the intention to reflect the mood of the book rather than create a literal depiction of it (pp. 104–5). Illustration was also seen as a way of breathing new life into otherwise tired titles.

Straightforward – rather than manipulated – photography was introduced during Alan Aldridge's time as Art Director and gave the covers a certain realism, but in the process they lost much of their mystery. That process continued under Pelham and beyond. So obvious was the idea behind the cover photograph on many titles that the most memorable feature was the distinctive typographic treatment used for the author's name.

The John Franklin Bardin Omnibus, 1976. Cover photograph by Paul Wakefield.

The Silent Partner, 1978. The cover design incorporates scenes from the Mario Kassar, Andrew Vajna presentation of a Joel B. Michaels, Garth H. Drabinsky, Stephen Young production, *The Silent Partner*.

Education, 1971–2

David Pelham commissioned Derek Birdsall's company Omnific to give the whole of the Education series a new look in 1971. Previous designs had stressed particular subject areas with colour coding and patterns, but Birdsall kept unity across the whole range by using white backgrounds and black type, emphasizing their individuality by using varying sizes of the bold sans serif typeface Railroad Gothic, as large as the spine allowed. Ranged right to a common line, it gave the series considerable bookshelf presence.

The front covers used strong typography with graphic humour to illustrate the content of each book. Working closely with Charles Clarke, Penguin Education's editor, Omnific handled the production and artwork for over 200 titles and commissioned thirty other designers to work on many of them.

When the size of the books was enlarged to the B format the spine alignment of the typography was retained, which ensured continuity.

Penguin by Design

The City, 1977. Cover design:
Omnific/Philip Thompson.

Inflation, 1972. Cover design:
Omnific/Derek Birdsall.

Management of Change &
Conflict, 1972. Cover design:
Omnific/Derek Birdsall.

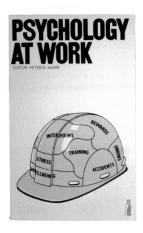

Psychology at Work, 1978.
Cover design: Jones Thompson.

Human Ageing, 1972. Cover
design: Omnific/Derek Birdsall.

What's the Use of Lectures?,
1974. Cover design: Omnific/
Stephen Scales.

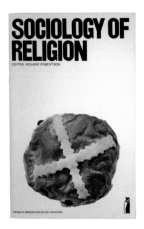

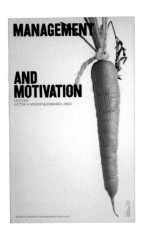

Sociology of Religion, 1976.
Cover design: Omnific/
Martin Causer.

Learner Teacher, 1972. Cover
design: Omnific/Martin Causer.

Management and Motivation,
1979. Cover design: Omnific/
Derek Birdsall.

Erving Goffman
Encounters

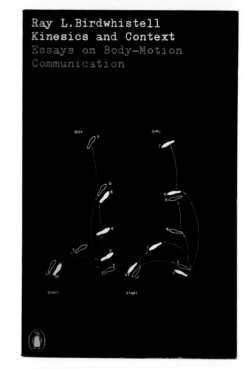

Ray L.Birdwhistell
Kinesics and Context
Essays on Body-Motion
Communication

Stephan Körner
Fundamental Questions
of Philosophy

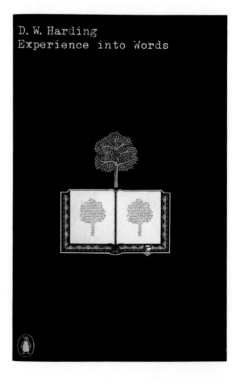

D. W. Harding
Experience into Words

Keith Thomas
Religion and the Decline
of Magic

University titles, 1972

Pelham commissioned John McConnell (who joined Pentagram in 1972) to design the university range of titles produced by Penguin Education. To differentiate them from the general Education titles designed by Derek Birdsall, the university titles featured black covers with an understated typography – typewriter (curiously, a Birdsall favourite: see the John Updike titles, p. 171) – and simple line drawings that directly illustrated each title.

Religion and the Decline of Magic, 1971. Designed by John McConnell.

OPPOSITE: *Encounters*, 1972. Designed by John McConnell.

Kinesics and Context, 1973. Designed by John McConnell.

Normality and Pathology in Childhood, 1973. Designed by John McConnell.

Anna Freud
Normality and Pathology
in Childhood

OPPOSITE: *Fundamental Questions of Philosophy*, 1973. Designed by John McConnell.

Experience into Words, 1974. Designed by John McConnell.

Library of Physical Sciences

Another of the Education department's sub-series was designed by Lock/Pettersen Ltd. They featured a consistent area containing the name of the series and the Penguin Education logo, below which was the title and author name. The sans serif type used was Univers rather than Helvetica, which had almost become the Penguin standard since the early 1960s.

The lower two thirds of each cover featured a simple design of geometric elements creating a pattern suggestive of the subject matter and making effective use of the two colours in which each cover was printed.

OPPOSITE: *Free-Electron Physics*, 1970. Cover design by Lock/Pettersen Ltd.

Orbitals and Symmetry, 1970. Cover design by Lock/Pettersen Ltd.

Nuclear Reactions, 1971. Cover design by Lock/Pettersen Ltd.

OPPOSITE: *Gases, Liquids and Solids*, 1969. Cover design by Cummings Lock & Pettersen.

Quantum Chemistry, 1972. Cover design by Lock/Pettersen Ltd.

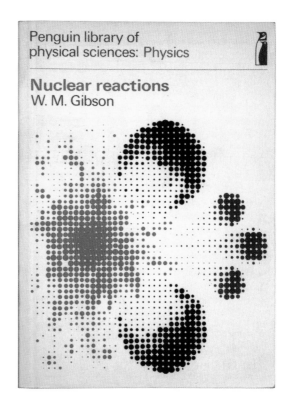

Penguin library of physical sciences: Physics

Free-electron physics
P.S. Farago

Penguin library of physical sciences: Chemistry

Orbitals and symmetry
D. S. Urch

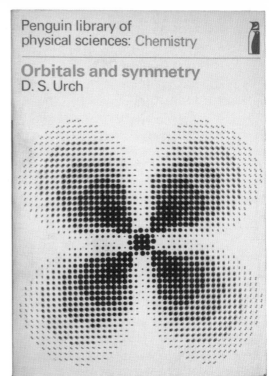

The Penguin library of physical sciences: Physics/Chemistry

Gases, liquids and solids
D. Tabor

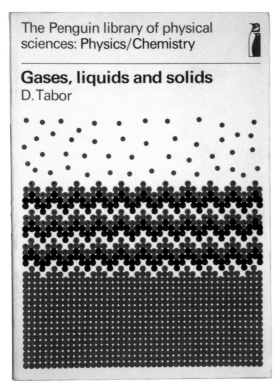

Penguin library of physical sciences: Chemistry

Quantum chemistry
D. A. Brown

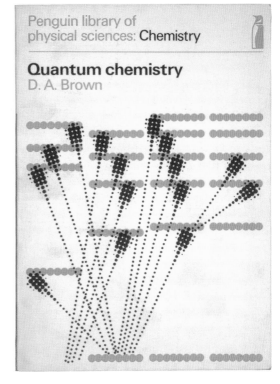

Mel Calman

The Costs of Economic Growth, 1969. Cover design by Mel Calman.

Calman, born in 1931, studied at St Martin's School of Art and made his name as a 'pocket' gag cartoonist for the national papers. His career, spanning the late 1950s to his death in 1994, took in the *Daily Express*, the *Sunday Telegraph*, the *Observer*, the *Sunday Times* and *The Times*, as well as a great deal of auxiliary work.

There used to be a perception that books on serious subjects had to have serious covers, and Pelican, in commissioning illustrations by Mel Calman for their titles, played an important role in changing that prejudice. The use of Calman's cartoons reinforced the Pelican approach – to commission accessible books on serious topics – and undoubtedly gave them greater appeal. Although visually different from the rest of the Pelican covers, they share the same idea-based approach to illustrating the title and, with their economy of line, do not feel out of place. In 1968 Penguin published a collection of his cartoons as *The Penguin Mel Calman*.

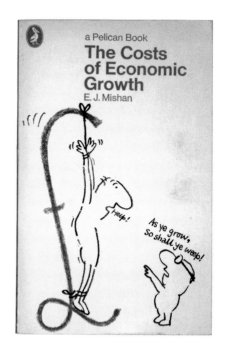

The Age of Automation, 1966. Cover design by Mel Calman and Graham Bishop.

Penguin by Design

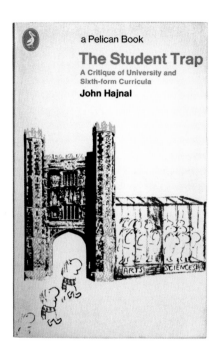

Business Adventures, 1971.
Cover design by Mel Calman
and Philip Thompson.

The Student Trap, 1972.
Cover design by Mel Calman
and Philip Thompson.

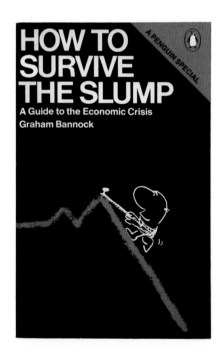

How to Survive the Slump, 1975.
Cover design by Mel Calman.

The Juggernauts, 1973.
Cover design by Mel Calman
and Philip Thompson.

Pelican swansong

The strong cover designs for Pelican
books – which had begun with the John
Curtis covers of the late 1950s (pp. 92–3)
– continued into the 1970s. The Marber
grid survived on Pelicans longer than
for crime or fiction, and even when it
was abandoned, Pelican layouts did
not change dramatically. Under David
Pelham, the typography continued in an
asymmetric arrangement of Helvetica
in the upper third of the cover, with the
Pelican logo in one of the top corners.

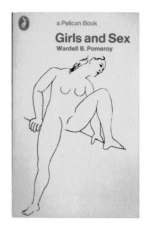

Even more than previously, simple
graphic ideas were favoured, with photographs used occasionally as appropriate.
There was an element of maturity and
less experimentation with the printing,
and when a particular technique such
as overprinting was used – for the R. D.
Laing titles, for example (pp. 192–3) –
it was principally for its ability to express an idea rather than simply for
visual effect.

Drugs and Human Behaviour,
1972. Cover design by Diagram.

Violent Men, 1972.
Cover design by Patrick McCreeth
(photograph John Hybert,
Stroboscopic equipment by Dawe
Instruments Ltd).

**Marital
Breakdown**
J. Dominian

**J.K.Galbraith
Economics
and the
Public Purpose**

Dying
John Hinton

Marital Breakdown, 1982.
Cover design by Patrick McCreeth.

*Economics and the Public
Purpose*, 1975. Cover design by
Derek Birdsall.

Dying, 1979.
Cover design by Michael Morris.

**The Complete
Plain Words**

Sir Ernest Gowers

Homosexuality
D. J. West

**Venereal
Diseases**
R. S. Morton

The Complete Plain Words, 1983.
Cover design by David Pelham.

Homosexuality, 1974.
Cover design by Michael Morris.

Venereal Diseases, 1974.
Cover design by Michael Morris.

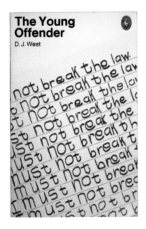

**The Young
Offender**
D. J. West

Yoga
Ernest Wood

Income Distribution
Jan Pen

The Young Offender, 1974.
Cover design by Jones Thompson
Ireland.

Yoga, 1974. Cover photograph
by Barry Lategan.

Income Distribution, 1974.
Cover design by Brian Delaney.

Alcoholism, 1979. Cover
photograph by Philip Webb.

Anxiety and Neurosis, 1976.
Cover design by Michael Morris.

Communications, 1982.
Cover design by Carole Ingham.

Education, 1976.
Cover design by Alan Fletcher.

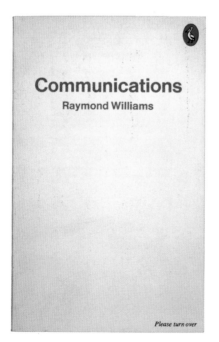

Penguin by Design

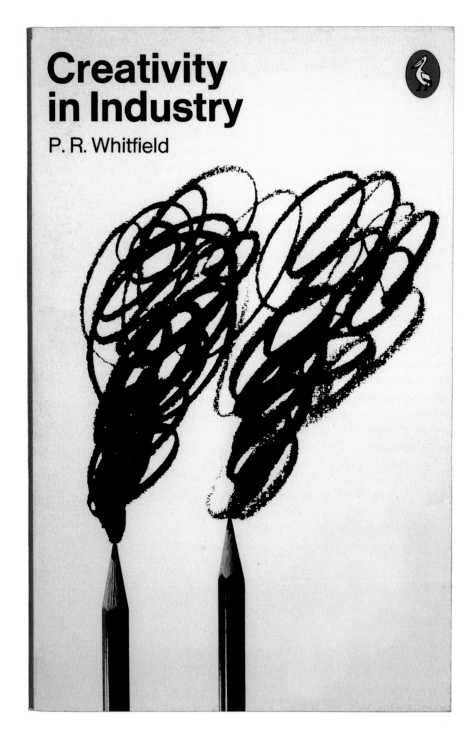

Creativity in Industry, 1975.
Cover design by David Pelham.

Self and Others, 1975. Cover
design by Germano Facetti.

The Divided Self, 1974. Cover design by Martin Bassett.

Science fiction

Apeman, Spaceman, 1972. Cover design by David Pelham.

David Pelham's early designs for the science fiction series continued the use of strongly coloured illustrations and black backgrounds introduced by Alan Aldridge. For some series, the typographic arrangement of series name, author and title did not vary, but specific typefaces were chosen to go with particular illustrative styles or individual authors (this spread and p. 196).

By the 1980s, this consistency was no longer adhered to (p. 197). While the airbrush fantasy illustrations followed the established tradition, they became difficult to appreciate because the typography was allowed to become too large and so competed for attention. A science fiction logo was introduced and awkwardly placed alongside the wording, further disturbing the balance.

Black Easter or *Faust Aleph-Null*, 1972. Cover design by David Pelham.

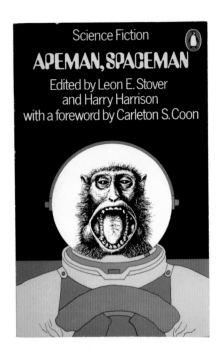

Penguin by Design

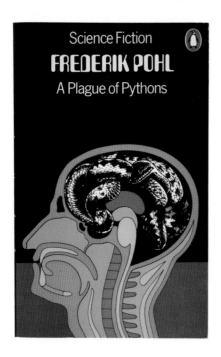

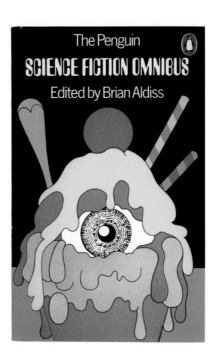

A Plague of Pythons, 1973.
Cover design by David Pelham.

The Penguin Science Fiction Omnibus, 1973. Cover design by David Pelham.

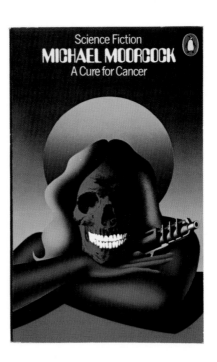

The Space Merchants, 1973.
Cover design by David Pelham.

A Cure for Cancer, 1973.
Cover design by David Pelham.

The Terminal Beach, 1974. Cover
illustration by David Pelham.

The Drowned World, 1976. Cover
illustration by David Pelham.

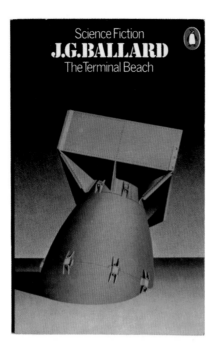

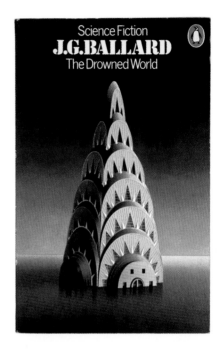

*The Four-Dimensional
Nightmare*, 1977. Cover
illustration by David Pelham.

The Drought, 1977. Cover
illustration by David Pelham.

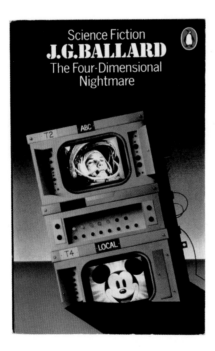

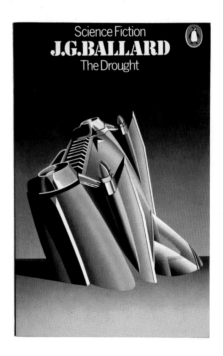

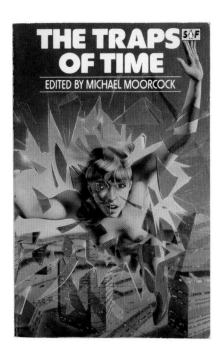

The Traps of Time, 1979.
Cover illustration by Adrian
Chesterman.

Tiger! Tiger!, 1979.
Cover illustration by Adrian
Chesterman.

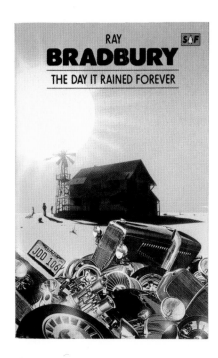

Search the Sky, 1979.
Cover illustration by Adrian
Chesterman.

The Day It Rained Forever,
1984. Cover illustration by
Adrian Chesterman.

Modern European Poets, early 1970s

Begun in 1965, this series featured portraits of the authors as a key element of its cover designs. Over time a variety of treatments were used to keep these covers looking interesting and to help unify images which came from a variety of sources and could be of variable quality. Techniques included combining halftone photographs; reducing photographs to high-contrast versions and printing each in a different colour; and tracing photographs to create simple line drawings. As with all Facetti covers, the typography is set in Helvetica in a standard pattern.

Penguin Modern Poets, Volume 25 (pp. 200–201), a new look, 1975

Photography had featured prominently on this series since its inception in 1963. The series featured many photographic styles, initially understated, delicate, and almost abstract. Volume 25 marked something of a new beginning, with larger type and a single close-up image across back and front. The power of this look was not employed for long; the photography returned to landscapes, and the series ended with Volume 27 in 1979. Modern Poets reappeared in 1995 with numbering starting again at 1.

Three Czech Poets, 1971. The cover, designed by Sylvia Clench, shows: large detail, Vitězslau Nezval; above, Antonín Bartušek; below, Josef Hanzlik (photographs by Dilia, Prague).

OPPOSITE: *Selected Poems* (Abba Kovner and Nelly Sachs), 1971. The cover, designed by Sylvia Clench, shows: large detail, Nelly Sachs; small detail, Abba Kovner.

Selected Poems (Guillevic), 1974. Cover design by Sylvia Clench.

Selected Poems (Sándor Weöres and Ferenc Juhász), 1970. The cover shows: large detail, Sándor Weöres; small detail, Ferenc Juhász.

OPPOSITE: *Selected Poems* (Johannes Bobrowski and Horst Bienek), 1971. The cover, designed by Sylvia Clench, shows: large detail, Horst Bienek; small detail, Johannes Bobrowski.

Selected Poems (Paavo Haavikko and Tomas Tranströmer), 1974. Cover design by Sylvia Clench.

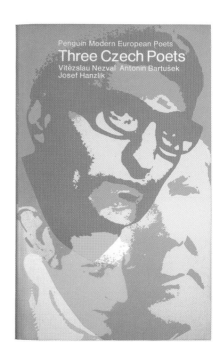

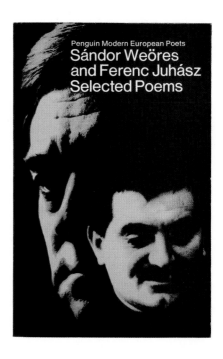

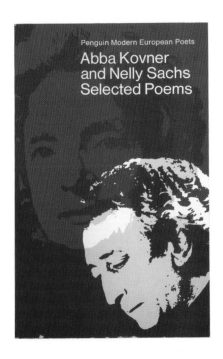

Penguin Modern European Poets

Abba Kovner
and Nelly Sachs
Selected Poems

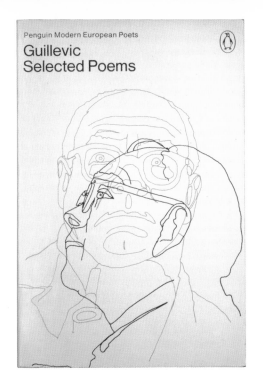

Penguin Modern European Poets

Guillevic
Selected Poems

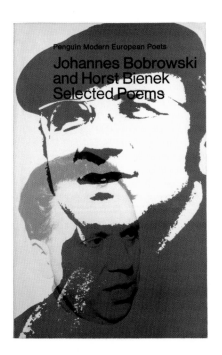

Penguin Modern European Poets

Johannes Bobrowski
and Horst Bienek
Selected Poems

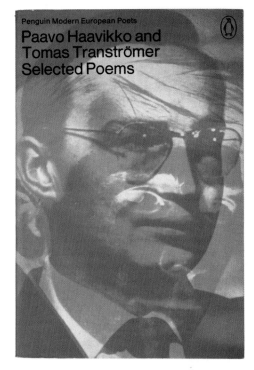

Penguin Modern European Poets

Paavo Haavikko and
Tomas Tranströmer
Selected Poems

Penguin Modern Poets is a series designed to introduce contemporary poetry to the general reader by publishing representative work by each of three modern poets in a single volume. In each case the selection has been made to illustrate the poet's characteristics in style and form.

Cover photograph by Harri Peccinotti

United Kingdom 45p
Australia $1.55 (recommended)
New Zealand $1.55
Canada $1.75
U.S.A. $1.75

Poetry
ISBN 0 14
042.181 5

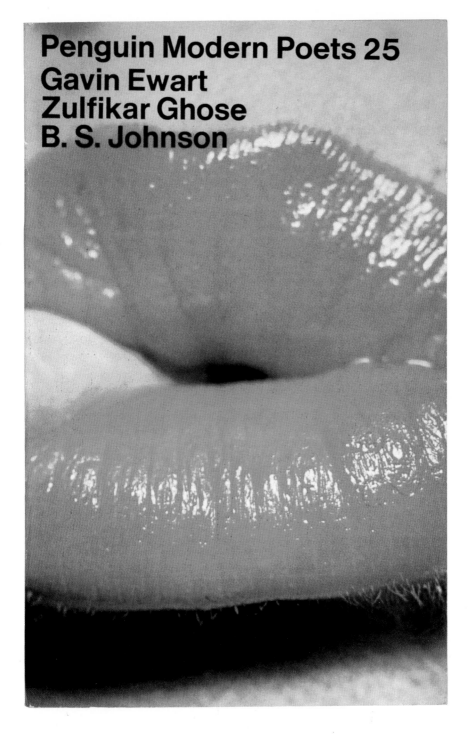

Penguin Modern Poets 25
Gavin Ewart
Zulfikar Ghose
B. S. Johnson

Penguin Modern Poets, Volume
25 (back and front cover),
1975. Cover photograph by
Harri Peccinotti.

New Penguin Shakespeare, 1980

When David Pelham came to redesign
the New Penguin Shakespeare in 1980,
like Facetti he too felt the need to make
the various titles distinct from each other.

Pelham commissioned Paul Hogarth,
who had previously illustrated a series
of titles by Graham Greene (pp. 174–5).
The translucence of his watercolours
provides a clear break from the previous
series design (pp. 152–3), but the effect
is somewhat spoilt by the fussy typography above.

In this design typography is used to
suggest the Elizabethan period, broken-
script lettering combining with copper-
plate flourishes. In terms of hierarchy,
Shakespeare has become the most important element again, fragmenting the
series title and reducing the space for the
title of the play itself. The quality of the
'Shakespeare' lettering is let down by
the weight of the rules above and below,
which are too heavy, and on certain
covers (*The Merchant of Venice* and *A
Midsummer Night's Dream*) the close
letter-spacing of the Garamond capitals
in the play's title is unfortunate.

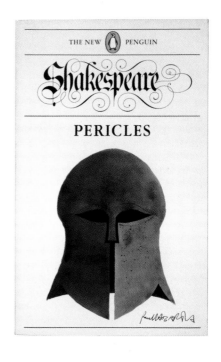

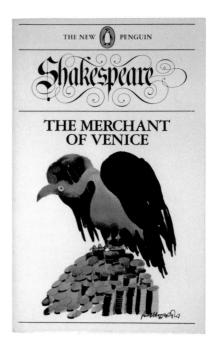

Penguin by Design

THE NEW PENGUIN

Shakespeare

A MIDSUMMER
NIGHT'S DREAM

A Midsummer Night's Dream, 1980. Cover illustration by Paul Hogarth.

The Best of Bee Nilson
ISBN 0 14
046.272 4

Jane Grigson Fish Cookery
ISBN 0 14
046.276 3

Jane Grigson English Food
ISBN 0 14
046.243 0

Tom Stobart Herbs, Spices and Flavourings
ISBN 0 14
046.261 9

Macnicol Hungarian Cookery
ISBN 0 14
046.240 6

Ross and Waterfield Leaves from our Tuscan Kitchen
ISBN 0 14
046.253 8

Grigson The Mushroom Feast
ISBN 0 14
046.273 2

Anna Thomas The Vegetarian Epicure
ISBN 0 14
046.201 5

Mince Matters — Elaine Hallgarten

Cookery, 1970s

The wide-ranging cookery list – which formed part of the Handbooks series – was given a unified appearance in the 1970s by the use of photography extending over both covers and spine. On a shelf, either in the bookshop or in the home, this made for a striking display, and the pictures on the front allowed the title to be 'read' instantly from the image alone. There was therefore no need for any suggestive typography: initially the uncompromisingly straightforward Facetti principles were followed.

On some titles, this disciplined approach was allowed to lapse, and intrusively positioned 'homely' serif typefaces started to appear (*Cordon Bleu Desserts and Puddings*).

Mince Matters, 1979. Cover photograph by Robert Golden.

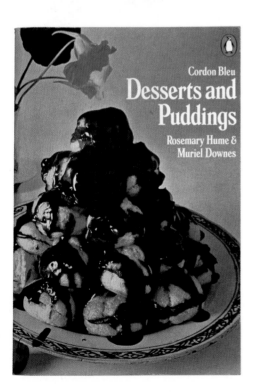

Cordon Bleu — **Desserts and Puddings** — Rosemary Hume & Muriel Downes

Cordon Bleu Desserts and Puddings, 1976. Cover photograph by Alan and Freda Spain.

Specials: the end of the line

Specials continued as a series into the 1980s but seemed to have lost their way. Originally their success had been built upon a combination of topical and urgent subject matter, good writing, speed of production and an absence of competition. The growth of newspaper consumption and television finally led to their demise.

While the published titles continued to reflect the key issues of British and world politics, the cover designs seem to suggest a lack of interest within the company. They have neither the conviction nor the consistency of previous covers (pp. 28–31 and 112–15). Of those shown here, only *The Homeless and the Empty Houses* really combines text and image into a powerful composition, but even that is marred by the insensitive 'Special' corner tab. The others feature obvious visual ideas presented by ordinary and uninteresting graphic means, a sad end for a series that had so significantly contributed to Penguin's initial success.

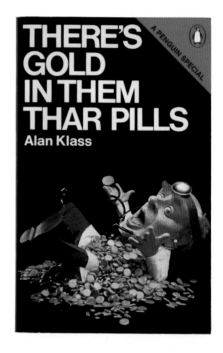

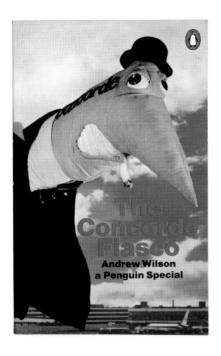

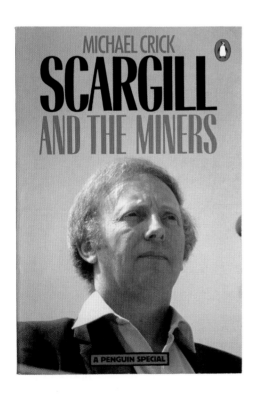

Lace, 1983. Cover photograph
by Allen Vogel.

*The Fall and Rise of Reginald
Perrin*, 1979.
The cover photograph shows
Leonard Rossiter in the title role
of the BBC Television series *The
Fall and Rise of Reginald Perrin*,
produced and directed by Gareth
Gwenlan. BBC Copyright photo-
graph by David Edwards. Cover
design by Mick Keates.

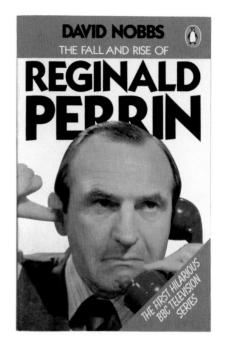

More of the Good Life, 1977.
The cover shows Richard Briers,
Felicity Kendal and Penelope
Keith in the BBC-TV production
of *The Good Life*, produced
by John Howard Davies. BBC
copyright photograph by David
Edwards. Cover lettering by
Shirtsleeve Studios.

Absolute Beginners, 1986.
Photograph: Davies and Starr.
Cover design by Tracy Dew.

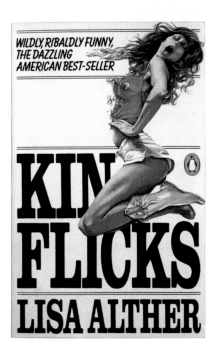

TV tie-ins and airport foil, 1970s and 1980s

Since the 1950s the company had gladly taken advantage of any opportunity to 'tie-in' a book with a television programme or film. But the demands of marketing departments and production companies meant that their covers were never elegant combinations of text and image. The Penelope Keith inset on *More of the Good Life* and the triangular flash on *The Fall and Rise of Reginald Perrin* mar what would otherwise be acceptable compositions.

Nothing, though, can excuse the mixture of conflicting elements on *Absolute Beginners*.

In the search for bestsellers, many more covers than before were aimed squarely at popular taste. *Kinflicks* is often cited as an example of this, but given its subject matter it is hard to imagine a tasteful cover. *Lace* is more typical of the genre, cliché photography and typography screaming for attention at the airport newsstand. *Money* at first glance seems to be of the same ilk – gratuitous use of foil-blocking and lurid soft-focus imagery – but *Money*'s cover is an illustration of the story itself, not a come-on in the same sense at all.

Kinflicks, 1984. Cover illustration by Cathy Wyatt.

Money, 1987.

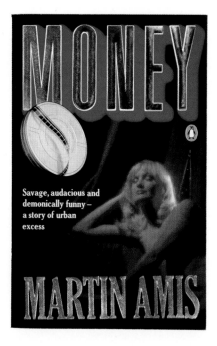

New King Penguins, 1981

The Farewell Party, 1984. Cover
illustration by Andrzej
Klimowski.

OPPOSITE: The Infernal Desire
Machines of Doctor Hoffman,
1982. Cover illustration by
James Marsh.

The Slow Train to Milan, 1985.
Cover illustration by
John Clementson.

The Joke, 1987. Cover
illustration by Andrzej Klimowski.

OPPOSITE: The Bloody Chamber,
1987. Cover illustration by
James Marsh.

The Heart is a Lonely Hunter,
1983. Cover illustration by
Nick Bantock.

Among collectors and lovers of Penguin
history there was much disquiet about the
resurrection of the King Penguin name
for a series of contemporary literature.

The basic design of these was by Ken
Carroll and Mike Dempsey and featured
an inset panel containing the series title
(in Century Bold Condensed) on both
cover and the white spine. Commissioned
illustrations played a prominent role
in the series, and Andrzej Klimowski's
covers for Milan Kundera's titles are jus-
tifiably well known. They are, however,
only one example of a variety of styles
which were used on covers in a series that
continued for nine years. Unfortunately –
as with the science fiction covers shown
on p. 197 – the typography of author and
title is often intrusive.

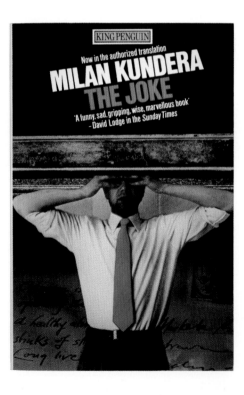

KING PENGUIN

ANGELA CARTER
The Infernal Desire
Machines of
Doctor Hoffman

KING PENGUIN

LISA ST AUBIN
DE TERÁN

THE SLOW TRAIN
TO MILAN

'MAGICAL...EXHILARATING...CONFIRMS THE PROMISE
SHOWN BY HER FIRST NOVEL, 'KEEPERS OF THE HOUSE'
– GUARDIAN

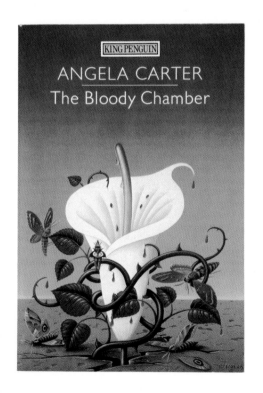

KING PENGUIN

ANGELA CARTER
The Bloody Chamber

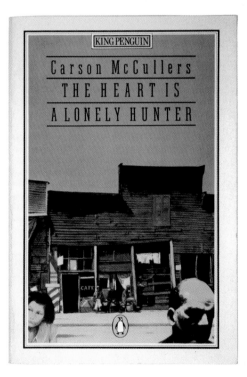

KING PENGUIN

Carson McCullers
THE HEART IS
A LONELY HUNTER

CAFE

Reference

Reference titles had been produced
under that series name by Penguin since
1944, the first being *A Dictionary of
Science*, by E. B. Uvarov, which had
originally appeared as a Special in 1942.
By the 1980s the list had grown to include a range of titles related to the use
of language as well as dictionaries and
reference books on many other subjects.

From the early 1970s a series of
cover designs was provided by Omnific.
These followed the pattern they had already used on the Education titles (pp.
180–81): strong typography with an emphasis on a keyword from the title and a
visual or typographic play on the subject
matter as the supporting illustration.

The 1980s redesign was by Ken
Carroll and Mike Dempsey and featured
prominent typography of a more polite
kind. 'Modern' typefaces (i.e. seriffed
with an extreme contrast between thick
and thin stems) had become fashionable,
and Century Bold Condensed is used in
a formal centred arrangement above an
illustration. The basic structure of this
design lasted until 1997, when the background colour was changed to black
and a more prominent use of orange
branding was introduced. The typeface
used for the title on later books reverted
to a condensed sans serif, which gave
the spines, particularly, more impact.

THE PENGUIN
DICTIONARY OF
ECONOMICS

GRAHAM BANNOCK, R. E. BAXTER
AND EVAN DAVIS

NEW EDITION

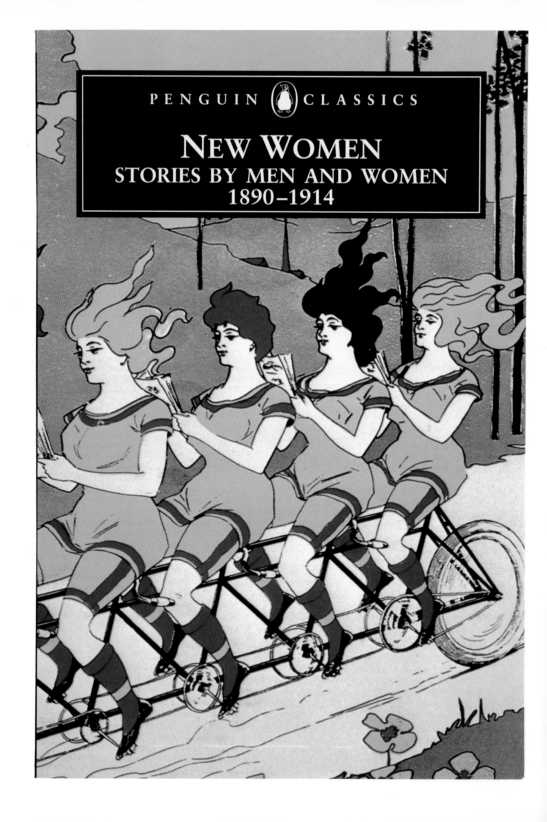

PENGUIN CLASSICS

NEW WOMEN
STORIES BY MEN AND WOMEN
1890–1914

Penguin Classics, 1985

On 29 August 1985 a new design for the Classics series was introduced with fifteen new titles, twenty-one reissues and fifty-eight reprints. By December a further 205 titles had been repackaged.

The new design by Art Director Steve Kent has none of the tension between old and new which characterized the previous 'black' design of Facetti. Instead Kent sought to play up the 'classic' feel with formal typography, and in that respect it recalls the 1950s covers. The design features the typeface Sabon, centred rather tightly, white within a black panel. Imagery is either used as a complete background or occupies the area below, and butting up against, the title panel.

One shudders to think what Jan Tschichold (designer of Sabon) would have made of its letterspacing on these covers. Compare these with his own revision of the Classics from 1947 (p. 65).

Another element of the design borrowed from the original classics was the use of colour coding – in the form of narrow strips at the top of the spine – to denote the origin of the contents: red for British and American; yellow for European; purple for classical; and green for oriental.

Dracula, 1993.
The cover photograph shows Henry Irving as Mephistopheles from the collections of the Theatre Museum by courtesy of the Board of Trustees of the Victoria and Albert Museum, London.

Sagas of Warrior-Poets, 2002.
The cover shows an illuminated initial letter from *Jónsbók* with a sailing scene, early 14th-century Icelandic manuscript © Stofnun Árna Magnússonar á Islandi, Reykjavik [GKS 3269a 4to].

OPPOSITE: *New Women*, 2002.
Cover photo © Hulton Archive.

Originals, 1989

Men Behaving Badly, 1989. Cover illustration by Dirk Van Dooren. Cover design by the Senate.

OPPOSITE: *Blood and Water*, 1989. Cover illustration by Robert Mason. Cover designed by the Senate.

Jaguars Ripped My Flesh, 1989. Cover photography by Michael Trevillion. Cover designed by the Senate.

The Fourth Mode, 1989. Cover Illustration by Andrzej Klimowski. Cover design by the Senate.

OPPOSITE: *On Extended Wings*, 1989. Cover design by the Senate. Cover photo by David Fairman.

Cambodia, 1989. Cover photography by Robert Shackleton & Richard Baker. Cover designed by the Senate.

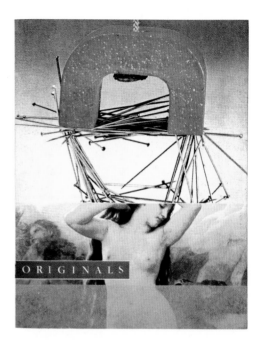

Once illustration was allowed on to Penguin front covers in the 1950s, there were only a few titles which did not use some pictorial element as part of their layout. Until 1989, however, there were no covers which had attempted to leave both author and title off the front.

Like the 1981 King Penguin titles, Originals were a series showcasing contemporary fiction. Their design, by the Senate, was different in nearly every respect. The size was non-standard (shorter than A format but as wide as B); the only type on the front cover was the word 'Originals' in a box that continued onto the spine; they were the first Penguin covers to be matt-laminated, with flaps and printing inside; and there was no Penguin logo on the front.

Such self-consciousness didn't last, however: only the original titles appeared in this pure form, and sales were so disappointing that the design was reworked in a more conventional manner (bottom three covers). Unsold copies of the first titles were re-covered and all subsequent books carried the amended design. The series later changed size to a standard B format, though a couple of titles were produced as A5.

The problems with the type and format detract from an otherwise brave attempt to use continuous illustration on back and front covers with a recognizable series style. This series also continued a practice, begun with Hans Schmoller's commissioning of David Gentleman and others in the 1950s, of using illustrators – such as Dirk Van Dooren and Daryl Rees – barely out of college.

Penguin by Design

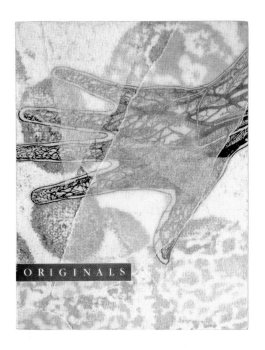

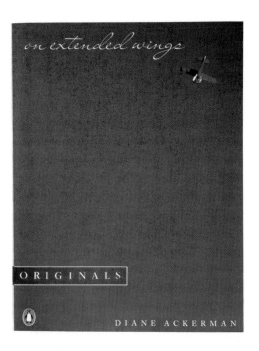

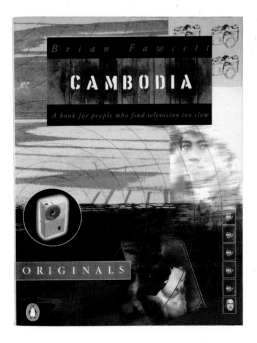

Penguin 60s, 1995

Essays on Dolls, 1994.

Penguin's 60th anniversary occurred in 1995, and it was celebrated by the publication of two series – orange-branded fiction and non-fiction followed shortly afterwards by black Classics – of 60 miniature books which sold for 60 pence (a figure that meant very slim profits). Their smaller size (just 138 × 105 mm) was similar to that of the Syrens series (*Essays on Dolls*), published with little fanfare in the previous year. Penguin 60s had differing content – some comprised extracts, some were complete texts – and their extent varied from 54 to 92 pages.

Classics 60s looked like miniature versions of the 1985 Classics design – with the same spacing problems already discussed (p. 215) – but featured different illustrations from those on the standard books. The orange 60s had a quite different appearance from their full-size equivalents, with full-bleed cover images and centred text set in the Trajan typeface, with the author surname larger than first name, the title smaller than both.

The Emperor's New Clothes, 1995. Cover illustration by Arthur Rackham (photo: Mary Evans Picture Library).

Following the success of the initial two series, a second series of orange 60s was launched but did not reach 60 titles; a set of 30 Puffin titles appeared as Penguin Children's 60s; and a series of Penguin Twentieth-Century Classics 60s was announced, but never materialized.

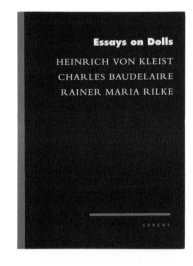

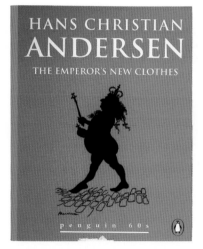

Penguin by Design

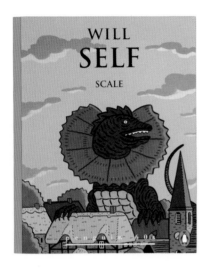

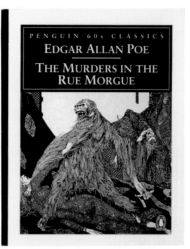

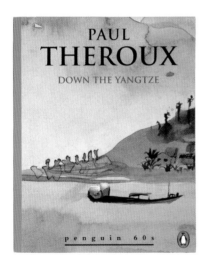

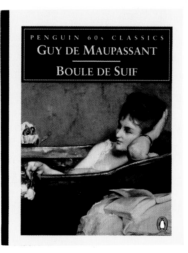

Scale, 1995.
Cover illustration by Jason Ford.

The Murders in the Rue Morgue, 1995. The cover shows an original illustration by Harry Clarke from *Tales of Mystery and Imagination* by Edgar Allan Poe, Harrap, 1919 (photo: Mary Evans Picture Library).

Down the Yangtze, 1995.
Cover illustration by Tim Vyner.

Boule de Suif, 1995.
The cover shows a detail from *The Bath* by Alfred Stevens in the Musée d'Orsay, Paris (photo: Girandon/Bridgeman Art Library).

V. Re-inventing the Brand, 1996–2005

Detail taken from *Sixty Stories*, 2005 (p. 237). Illustration by Vault 49.

V. Re-inventing the Brand, 1996–2005

John Hamilton

After the depression of the 1970s and 1980s and the uncertainties that followed, the Penguin group was in a state of disarray. Following the departure of Trevor Glover and the appointment of Anthony Forbes Watson as head of Penguin, Helen Fraser was appointed Managing Director. Previously MD at Reed, she brought with her several senior editors and an Art Director – John Hamilton.

It was decided at this time to split the adult side of the company into two parts: Penguin Press and Penguin General. The Press list is focused on serious non-fiction (including what would have been Pelicans), Classics and Reference, while General publishes literary and mass-market fiction and the more populist non-fiction titles (there is a certain amount of overlap, in fact).

Initially this reorganization was not reflected in Hamilton's Art Department, which had responsibility for both sides. When he arrived he found a comfortable commissioning policy that was fostering predictable design, and he was determined that that should change. He believed, like Aldridge and Pelham before him, that titles should be treated individually, and he was keen to use that freedom to attract a younger audience. To enable greater prominence to be placed on the individuality of the designs, Hamilton suggested dropping the orange spines from the majority of fiction titles and removing the ISBN from the spine. This simple loss of orange asserted the importance of design but angered many Penguin fans and collectors, who tend to revere such links with the company's origins. But while the colour branding had, in the past, been seen by book-buyers as a guarantee of quality, more recent experience suggested that it was having the reverse effect. With the books stripped of this once-reassuring colouring, the significance of editorial choices and the cover designs inspired by them became greater than ever.

Hamilton first started to create a stir with a small fiction series marketed loosely as 'Essentials', comprised of modern classics. Such unity as there was lay in the commissioning policy and choice of titles rather than any consistency of external appearance (pp. 226–9). The covers, which first appeared in 1998, elicited much press comment, both good and bad, but more importantly initiated the rebirth of a vibrant Penguin design culture.

Soon afterwards, the Art Department was split to reflect the editorial structure. John Hamilton moved to General and Pascal Hutton joined as Art Director of Press. While the contemporary fiction list continued to promote the individuality of each title, series such as the Classics and Twentieth-

Century Classics, housed in the Press division, were aimed at a different market, where the reassurance of a series style was, and still is, a great asset. Unhappy with the appearance of both lists, Hutton began to introduce changes. As the new millennium drew closer, and at the editor's request, Twentieth-Century Classics was returned to its original name of Modern Classics, with a restrained design by Jamie Keenan. Relying almost totally on images for impact, its success as a series is a tribute to brilliant picture research and commissioning within the company.

Jim Stoddart

But it was left to Hutton's successor, Jim Stoddart, who took over in September 2001, to instigate the overhaul of the Classics covers (pp. 234–5). He commissioned Angus Hyland of Pentagram to tackle the redesign, but the process was anything but straightforward: any big decisions regarding the Classics list have to be taken in conjunction with the US arm of the company, as they represent a sizeable part of Penguin's worldwide Classics market, and getting editors on both sides of the Atlantic to agree to a new basic template to be applied to over 1,000 titles took a great deal of effort and patience.

Other important and more-easily realized projects from Press under the art direction of Stoddart have included a relaunch of the Reference series (2003) (pp. 242–3), which, when seen among other publishers' titles of that genre, appears as fresh as the original ten Penguins must have done in 1935, and the Classics off-shoot 'Great Ideas' (2004) (pp. 244–5), whose covers offer a carefully crafted interpretation of over 2,000 years of lettering and typographic history.

Following the acceptance of the Macintosh as its main design and production platform, Penguin have made changes in the way the texts of their books are produced. The dedicated Text Design departments were closed in 2003 and most manuscripts are now set to follow one of a small number of standard designs that each division has determined upon ('standard grids'). Where text-design input is required, that is now under the control of the Production Department, a situation akin to the pre-war set-up.

Apart from the structural reorganization of the company during this most recent period there have been changes to Penguin imprints – such as the handing over of the 'national treasure' that is the Buildings of England series to Yale University Press in 2002 after 50 years of development – while the wider Pearson group has seen expansion through further acquisitions: Rough Guides in 1996 and Dorling Kindersley (DK) in 2000. These remain, editorially at least, separate companies whose design traditions have yet to

impinge on Penguin, but because Pearson are keen for relationships to grow between all its companies a major relocation of offices took place in 2001. DK staff and all the people from the Penguin Wrights Lane offices (editorial and art, but also sales, marketing, publicity and so on) moved to the newly refurbished former Shell Mex House, now known as 80 Strand. The warehouses and offices at Harmondsworth were closed in 2004, with the warehousing functions moving to the main Pearson distribution centre on the outskirts of Rugby.

But while reorganization, relocation and the unpredictable nature of the publishing business constantly test a company's ability to present a coherent image to the outside world, the issue of identity, which had been such a dilemma ten years ago, is no longer problematic. While the use of the orange spine is not felt to be a liability any more, neither is it much used. The Penguin logo itself, however, is a prized asset, being recognized as a publisher's mark all over the world. To reinforce its status Pentagram were given the job of analysing the constituent parts of the company and rationalizing their identities. Penguin and Puffin continue as separate brands for adult and children's publishing, and their logos have been redrawn (very subtly in the case of the penguin). The older imprints such as Allen Lane, Michael Joseph and Hamish Hamilton are now sub-brands of Penguin, with logos reflecting that status.

In seventy years of publishing history, design has been a central concern. At the outset it was important in giving identity, later it became essential to survival in a world of fierce competition – today it continues to play both of these roles. The success or otherwise of cover design can be hard to quantify, but Penguin has long prided itself on using the best designers, illustrators and photographers available, to give them a strong image and make their covers compulsive to buyers. The situation is no different in 2005; the current art directors and designers are upholding a distinguished tradition.

OPPOSITE: *White Teeth*, 2001. Cover illustration by Ali Campbell.

OPPOSITE: Zadie Smith's critically acclaimed debut novel set in North West London, *White Teeth*, sums up much about the current Penguin approach to cover design. The cover, with its forceful typography integrating title, author name and 'blurb', sits on a background illustration by Ali Campbell that continues round the spine on to the cover and extends over both inside covers. Colours dominate, while the recognizable imagery is just enough to locate the cultural background against which the story unfolds.

WHITE TEETH

'FUNNY, CLEVER ... AND A ROLLICKING GOOD READ' *INDEPENDENT*

THE TOP TEN BESTSELLER

ZADIE

'THE OUTSTANDING DEBUT OF THE NEW MILLENNIUM' *OBSERVER*

SMITH

Penguin Essentials, 1998

One of the first intentions of the new Penguin General Art Director, John Hamilton, was to reinvigorate the design of the fiction list. Key titles were selected as 'Essentials' and grouped as an informal series. Believing that they needed to appeal to new buyers whose disposable income was otherwise being spent on music and clothing, Hamilton commissioned leading illustrators and design groups to produce all-over designs of a kind first significantly seen on the Originals in 1989 (pp. 216–17). For Hamilton, the Penguin brand, as seen in the logo and orange spine, was something of a liability; the orange spine was abandoned for these and all his subsequent cover designs, while the logo was played down at every opportunity.

There is no obvious unity to these cover designs except the boldness of their execution, and the use of prominent designers and illustrators helped achieve that goal. It is a credit to the designs that the majority are still considered good sellers and remain in current use.

Lark Rise, [>1998]. Cover: details from photographs by Tessa Traeger.

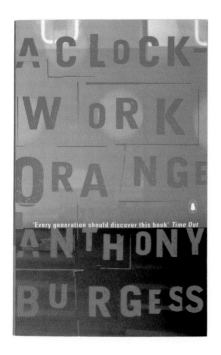

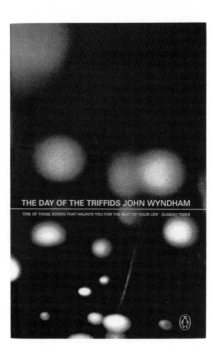

Hell's Angels, [>1998].
Design: Intro, London.

The Day of the Triffids, [>1998].
Photography by Lucinda Noble.

A Clockwork Orange, [>1998].
Photograph: Dirk Van Dooren.

Cat's Cradle, [>1998]. Cover
photography by Mike Venebles.

And the Ass Saw the Angel,
[>1998]. Cover by Banksy.
Photographed by Steve Lazarides.

Penguin by Design

Nineteen Eighty-Four, [>1998].
Cover photographs: Darren
Haggar, Dominic Bridges.

The Thirty-Nine Steps, [>1998].
Cover photo: © Images Colour
Library.

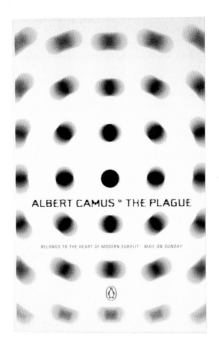

The Plague, [>1998].
[Cover design by gray318.]

Delta of Venus, [>1998].
Illustration: Paul Wearing.

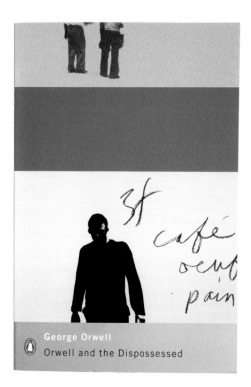 

Modern Classics, 2000

After a brief period of being known as Twentieth-Century Classics, Modern Classics returned with a new cover template by freelance designer Jamie Keenan. As in many other Penguin series designs combining type and image, the typographic element is restrained, being incorporated with the logo in a small silver panel. From the outset the intention was to use a variety of typefaces on these covers. Out of the initial list, only Trade Gothic, Franklin Gothic and Clarendon have been used to date, white for the author name and black for the title. The real job of animating the title and attracting the book-buying public falls to the image.

The role of illustration on titles such as these – mostly established works by widely regarded authors – is slightly different from that on new and contemporary titles seeking to make their presence felt for the first time. A wide range of imagery was, and still is, commissioned for this series. The George Orwell titles feature the work of Marion Deuchars and were widely praised when they first appeared:

The covers contain fragments of handwriting, bits of documentary photography and, in one case, a portion of the Union Jack … These, and other graphic elements, suggest a sure-footed understanding of Orwell's work, and provide the bookshop browser with what Stephen Bayley called a 'graphic haiku'.

(Shaughnessy, p. 21)

George Orwell Orwell's England

George Orwell Orwell in Spain

For other titles, the editors may decide that existing illustrations or photography may be a better approach, and in-house picture researchers will then be given the task of finding suitable material. The range of Modern Classics shown on the following pages demonstrates these varied strategies at work.

ABOVE: *Orwell's England*, 2001. Cover illustration by Marion Deuchars.

Orwell in Spain, 2001. Cover illustration by Marion Deuchars.

Evelyn Waugh A Handful of Dust

Anthony Burgess A Clockwork Orange

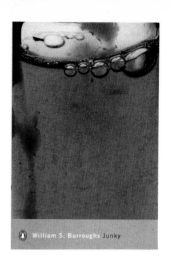

William S. Burroughs Junky

Norman Mailer The Fight

R. K. Narayan The Mahabharata

Nathanael West The Day of the Locust
and The Dream Life of Balso Snell

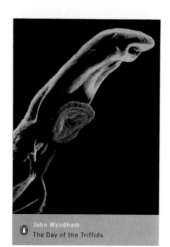

John Wyndham
The Day of the Triffids

F. Scott Fitzgerald The Great Gatsby

James Baldwin
Go Tell It on the Mountain

Hermann Hesse **Steppenwolf**

Federico García Lorca
The House of Bernarda Alba and Other Plays

Martin Amis **Money**

Damon Runyon **On Broadway**

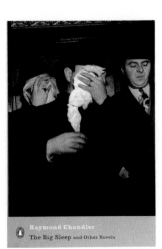

Raymond Chandler
The Big Sleep and Other Novels

Italo Svevo **Zeno's Conscience**

OPPOSITE: *A Handful of Dust*, 2000. The cover shows an original illustration for the journal *Gebrauchsgraphik*, April 1930 (photo: Martin Breese/Retrograph Archive).

A Clockwork Orange, 2000. Photography © Véronique Rolland.

Junky, 2002. Cover photo by Will Amlot.

The Fight, 2000. Cover photo of Ali in his training camp, Zaire, 1974 © Abbas/Magnum Photos.

The Mahabharata, 2001. Cover photo © Steve McCurry/ Magnum Photos.

The Day of the Locust, 2000. Cover photograph: *Torn Movie Poster*, 1930, by Walker Evans © Museum of Modern Art, New York.

The Day of the Triffids, 2001. Cover photograph © NCI/Science Photo Library.

The Great Gatsby, 2000. The cover shows *Untitled* (Bathing Suits by Izod) by George Hoyningen-Huene, from *Vogue*, July 5, 1930. Courtesy *Vogue*. Copyright © 1958 by Condé Nast Publications, Inc.

Go Tell It on the Mountain, 2001. Illustration: Natasha Michaels.

THIS PAGE: *Steppenwolf*, 2001. Cover photograph: *Untitled, Gellage No. II* (detail), 1989, by Michal Macku.

The House of Bernarda Alba, 2001. Cover: *Spanish Night* by Francis Picabia (1922), in the collection of the Museum Ludwig, Köln (photo: © Rheinisches Bildarchiv/ADAGP, Paris and DACS, London 2000).

Money, 2000. Photography © Images Colour Library.

On Broadway, 2000. Cover photography © Weegee ICP/Hulton Getty.

The Big Sleep, 2000. The cover shows *Arrested for Bribing Basketball Players*, New York, 1942 by Weegee © Hulton Getty.

Zeno's Conscience, 2002. Cover photography: Martin Scott-Jupp.

Penguin Classics, 2003

The latest design for the long-running
Classics series reflects a similar thinking
to that behind the Modern Classics
(pp. 230–33). These are image-led covers
with simple typography neatly contained
within a panel in the lower part. The
design was begun by Pentagram's Angus
Hyland, and original proposals featured
a ranged-left layout and the return of
Gill Sans to Penguin covers. But eventually the design was finished by Paul
Buckley of Penguin USA, who introduced a more centred design using the
typefaces Futura (Paul Renner, Germany,
1927) for the author and Mrs Eaves
(Zuzana Licko, USA, 1995) for the title.

The practice of using art contemporary with the literature in question was
begun by Germano Facetti in 1963
(pp. 124–5) and has been continued for
large parts of the current Classics list.
For these new titles images are key, with
a quality of reproduction that Facetti
could only have dreamed of when he initiated his redesign. But this approach is
no longer regarded as the only way to
treat the covers of classic literature. In
any case, after enlargement in 1985
when the English Library and other titles
were incorporated, there is now a far
more catholic interpretation of what actually constitutes a 'classic'. For certain
titles a departure from the norm has
taken place and existing contemporary
illustration has been used, such as
Chaperon Rouge by Vincent Burgeon
for the Brothers Grimm.

PENGUIN CLASSICS

AMMIANUS MARCELLINUS
The Later Roman Empire
(AD 354–378)

PENGUIN CLASSICS

MARY SHELLEY
Frankenstein

 PENGUIN CLASSICS

BROTHERS GRIMM

Selected Tales

Fiction today

A plurality of style characterizes the contemporary design of fiction, reflecting both the breadth of titles it represents, and the fact that this sector is fiercely competitive. Failure to succeed here would seriously jeopardise the finances of the whole company. In many ways covers today still utilize ideas first significantly introduced to Penguin by Alan Aldridge in 1965, but, because of the way the Penguin list is now organized, these approaches to marketing affect a greater proportion of the list than in his time.

Fiction is promoted in whatever way the editors, marketing department, and art director decide will best represent a particular title to the broadest potential readership. While this implies that cover designs are cleverly targeted at very specific audiences, and that there is no single dominant style employed, the aim – on the part of Art Director John Hamilton – to commission the best contemporary designers and illustrators ensures that a balance is usually struck between the needs of the market and design integrity.

Another difference between contemporary and previous practice lies in the approach to the company's identity. Where Pelham, in particular, was very concerned to remind book-buyers of the publisher's identity (by a consistent use and position of the logo, use of the orange spine, etc. (pp. 168–75)), today, that is seen as unnecessary. In general, if it is felt that a logo would disrupt the front cover design, it does not appear.

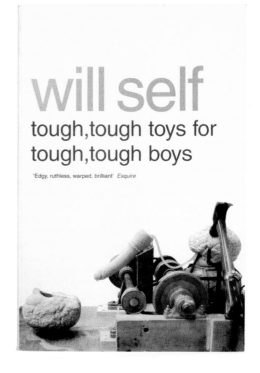

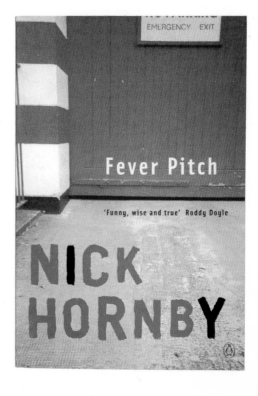

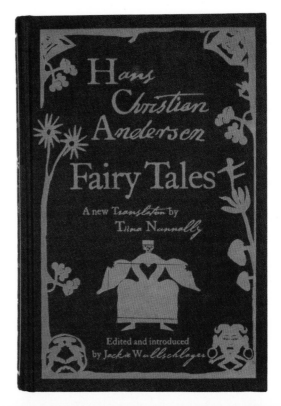

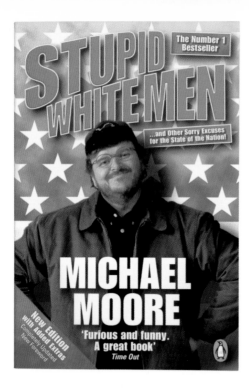

ABOVE: *Stupid White Men*, 2004.
[Cover design by Jim Stoddart.]

Terror Inc, 2003. [Cover design
by Coralie Bickford-Smith.]

RIGHT: *Americans*, 2003.
[Cover design by Jim Stoddart.]

OPPOSITE: *The Odyssey*, [>2000].
[The cover shows George
Clooney, Tim Blake Nelson and
John Turturro in Joel and Ethan
Coen's film, *O Brother, Where
Art Thou?*]

The Odyssey, 2001. Cover design:
gray318. Photography: © Jasper
James/Millennium Images.

Books for different markets: USA and classic texts

The way certain titles are marketed today differs considerably from fifteen years ago. A new century, closer links between different parts of the company, and developments in world politics generally, are some of the reasons for changes in the Penguin list. The United States is now an important market as well as being popular as subject matter. For two of the three covers shown here on the left, the cliché of American brashness is used to reflect the content of the titles, while *Terror Inc.* is reminiscent of the earlier 'graphic ideas' approach which underpinned nearly twenty years of Pelican cover design.

Other titles may appear with various covers in order to attract different kinds of readers. Homer's *Odyssey*, Penguin's original Classic from 1946, continues – in the Rieu translation – to be part of what the company refers to as 'black Classics' (pp. 234–5), but a quite different packaging of the same text aimed at a very different audience was produced as a film tie-in. There is also a newer (verse) translation by Robert Fagles – with stylish black and white photography on the cover – in a mini-series entitled 'Wonders of the World' alongside titles by Goethe, Virgil and Dante, among others.

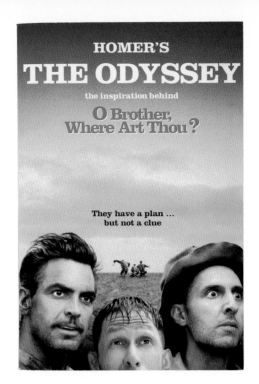

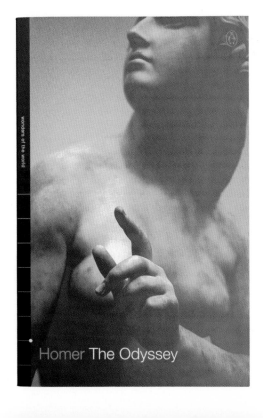

Angels, 2003. Jacket illustration: Mick Brownfield.

Books for different markets: 'chick lit' and non-fiction

An important part of the fiction list of recent years has been the genre commonly known as 'chick lit', contemporary fiction for – and often by – young women (*Angels* and *Spellbound*). For much of Penguin's history, designers have tried to combine effectiveness with a refined aesthetic, but when such an approach fails to address the visual sensibility of the intended audience, it founders. These covers – like *The Far Pavilions* in the 1980s – are very carefully calculated to appeal to potential readers.

With the demise of the Pelican imprint in 1991, titles which would once have formed part of that series now appear in the general Penguin list and are marketed with the same concern for title and lack of concern for identity (the four covers shown here on the right).

Spellbound, 2003. Illustration by Kirsten Ulve.

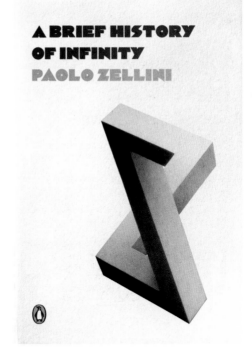

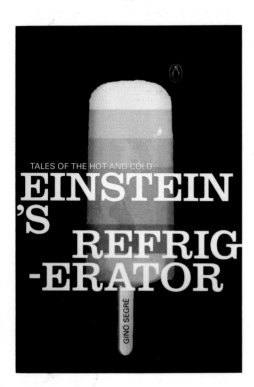

ABOVE: *Porcupines*, 2000.
Cover: photo of lodgepole pines
© Rod Planck/NHPA.

A Brief History of Infinity, 2005.
Cover design by David Pearson.

LEFT: *Einstein's Refrigerator*,
2004. Design: Steve Turner.

The Red Queen, 2000.
Designed at Yacht Associates.

Reference relaunch, 2003

While the fiction and General lists play on the difference between individual titles, the smaller, specialized series have always stressed brand identity.

The new cover designs for the Reference titles were a repackaging exercise replacing a look that had been introduced only four years before but which had dated horribly. The new look, by in-house designer David Pearson, combines allusions to Penguin's own history with a tactile element – rounded corners – giving them added bookshop appeal and greater durability.

The historical quotations come in the form of the horizontal tripartite division of the front cover, which gently recalls the 1935 covers, and the prominent use of spine typography, which recalls Derek Birdsall's work for the Penguin Education series in 1971 (pp. 180–81). Although the Penguin brand is strongly imposed on these titles, it is softened by the use of an illustrative element – or a colour for 'difficult' subjects – in the upper portion of the cover.

The typography reflects the fact that many series need to have the support of their American counterparts. Futura had been introduced for the Classics redesign in 2003 (pp. 234–5), and continuity into the reference list was thought desirable.

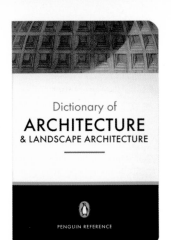

Dictionary of
ARCHITECTURE
& LANDSCAPE ARCHITECTURE

PENGUIN REFERENCE

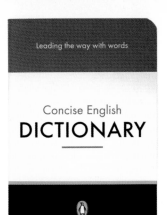

Leading the way with words

Concise English
DICTIONARY

PENGUIN REFERENCE

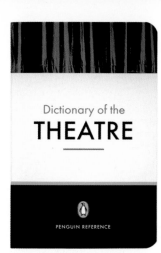

Dictionary of the
THEATRE

PENGUIN REFERENCE

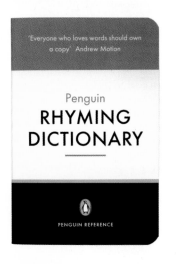

'Everyone who loves words should own
a copy' Andrew Motion

Penguin
**RHYMING
DICTIONARY**

PENGUIN REFERENCE

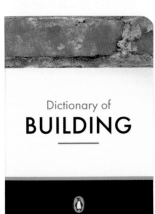

Dictionary of
BUILDING

PENGUIN REFERENCE

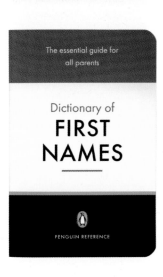

The essential guide for
all parents

Dictionary of
**FIRST
NAMES**

PENGUIN REFERENCE

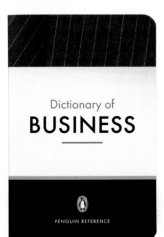

Dictionary of
BUSINESS

PENGUIN REFERENCE

The ultimate paperback
A–Z wordfinder

Concise
THESAURUS

PENGUIN REFERENCE

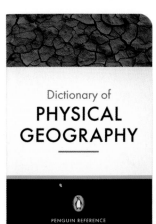

Dictionary of
**PHYSICAL
GEOGRAPHY**

PENGUIN REFERENCE

Great Ideas, 2004

Editorial Director Simon Winder came up with Great Ideas as a way of introducing a different readership to key texts that have helped shape civilization. Art Director Jim Stoddart handed responsibility for the design to David Pearson, who decided to let the flavour of each individual text influence the look of its cover.

Returning to the original A format and typographically led, each front cover gives the author and the title and includes a quote from the work in addition to the publisher and series name. Each is set in a manner suggestive of the lettering or typography of the time of the work's first publication. This gives the appearance in many cases of an old-fashioned title page, as though the book has no cover at all. Despite this great disparity of styles, the series is unified by being printed in the traditional printers' colours of black and red. The back cover and spine typography – in Dante – is consistent across all twenty titles. A tactile touch was added to the books by printing on an uncoated stock and by debossing the elements of the front cover.

The Art Director and designers for the series were nominated for the Design Museum's Designer of the Year Award in January 2005.

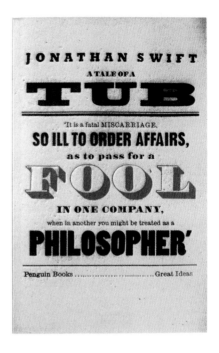

Meditations, 2004.
Cover artwork: Phil Baines.

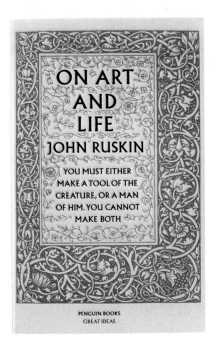

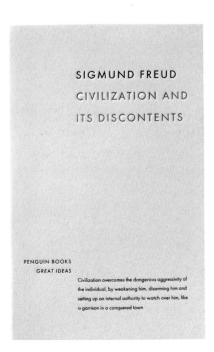

On Art and Life, 2004.
Cover artwork: David Pearson
at Penguin.

Civilization and Its Discontents,
2004. Cover artwork:
David Pearson at Penguin.

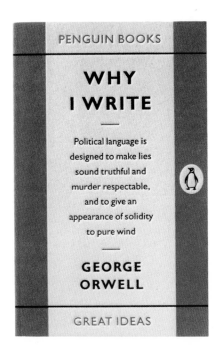

Confessions of a Sinner, 2004.
Cover artwork: Catherine
Dixon.

Why I Write, 2004.
Cover artwork: Alistair Hall at
We Made This.

TELEGRAMS AND CABLES:
PENGUINOOK, WEST DRAYTON

TELEPHONE
SKYPORT 1984 (7 LINES)
TELEX: 263130

PENGUIN BOOKS LTD

HARMONDSWORTH · MIDDLESEX

22 December 1965

Dear Mr Russ,

    What a glorious cover you
have done for the Graves.   Really
it makes the book worth buying
for its cover alone.   I do
congratulate you.

    Best wishes,

Anthony Godwin

Stephen Russ Esq
29 Shaw Hill
Melksham
Wiltshire

Chairman and Managing Director: SIR ALLEN LANE, HON.D.LITT., HON.LL.D., HON.M.A.
Deputy Managing Director: H.F.PAROISSIEN
Directors: THE RT HON. SIR EDWARD BOYLE, BT, M.P.   EUNICE FROST, O.B.E.
ANTHONY GODWIN   A.M.WALKER
Executive Directors: RONALD BLASS   CHARLES CLARK   CHRISTOPHER DOLLEY
J.A.HOLMES   R.C.INGRAM   DIETER PEVSNER   HANS SCHMOLLER

Bibliography and Sources

For the most comprehensive reading list on aspects of Penguin Books' history and development see
Graham, T., *Penguin in Print: A Bibliography*, London: Penguin Collectors' Society, 2003.

Books and magazine articles

Aynsley, J., & Lloyd Jones, L., *Fifty Penguin Years*, Harmondsworth: Penguin, 1985
Backemeyer, S. (ed.), *Picture This: The Artist as Illustrator*, London: A&C Black, 2005
Bailey, S., 'Ways of Working', *Dot Dot Dot*, 5, 2004
Baines, P., 'Face Lift: New Cuts at *The Times*', *Eye*, 40, summer 2001, pp. 52–9
Birdsall, D., *Notes on Book Design*, New Haven & London: Yale, 2003
Bradley, S., & Cherry, B. (eds.), *The Buildings of England: A Celebration*, London: Penguin Collectors' Society, 2001
Burbidge, P. G., & Gray, L. A., 'Penguin Panorama', *Printing Review*, Volume 20, No. 72, 1956, pp. 15–18
Cherry, B., *The Buildings of England: A Short History and Bibliography*, London: Penguin Collectors' Society, 1983
Cinamon, G. (ed.), 'Hans Schmoller, Typographer: His Life and Work', *The Monotype Recorder* (new series), 6, Salford: The Monotype Corporation, April 1987
Edwards, R. (ed.), *The Penguin Classics*, London: Penguin Collectors' Society (Miscellany 9), 1994
——, *A Penguin Collector's Companion*, London: Penguin Collectors' Society (revised edition), 1997
——, *Pelican Books, a Sixtieth Anniversary Celebration*, London: Penguin Collectors' Society (Miscellany 12), 1997
——, & Hare, S. (eds.), *Twenty-one Years*, London: Penguin Collectors' Society (Miscellany 10), 1995
Facetti, G., 'Paperbacks as a Mass Medium' (magazine unknown, probably US), pp. 24–9. The same text also appears as 'Penguin Books, London', *Interpressgrafik*, 1, 1969, pp. 26–41, with English translation on pp. 77–8
Frederiksen, E. Ellegaard, *The Typography of Penguin Books* (trans. K. B. Almlund), London: Penguin Collectors' Society, 2004
Greene, E., *Penguin Books: The Pictorial Cover 1960–1980*, Manchester Polytechnic, 1981
Hare, S., *Allen Lane and the Penguin Editors*, Harmondsworth: Penguin, 1996
——, '"Type-only Penguins Sell a Million" Shock', *Eye*, 54, winter 2004, pp. 76–7
Heller, S., 'When Paperbacks Went Highbrow: Modern Cover Design in the 1950s and 60s', *Baseline*, 43, 2003, pp. 5–12

Holland, S., *Mushroom Jungle: A History of Postwar Paperback Publishing*, Westbury: Zeon, 1993

Hollis, R., 'Germano Facetti: The Image as Evidence', *Eye*, 29, autumn 1998, pp. 62–9

Lamb, L., 'Penguin Books: Style and Mass Production', *Penrose Annual*, Volume 46, 1952, pp. 39–42

Lane, A., Fowler, D., *et al.*, *Penguins Progress, 1935–1960*, Harmondsworth: Penguin (Q25), 1960

McLean, R., *Jan Tschichold: Typographer*, London: Lund Humphries, 1975

McLuhan, E., quoted in posting of 13 October 2003 at www.brushstroke.tv/week03_35.html (weblog of Melanie Goux)

Moriarty, M. (ed.), *Abram Games: Graphic Designer*, London: Lund Humphries, 2003

Morpurgo, J. E., *Allen Lane: King Penguin*, London: Hutchinson, 1979

Peaker, C., *The Penguin Modern Painters: A History*, London: Penguin Collectors' Society, 2001

Pearson, J., *Penguins March On: Books for the Forces During World War II*, London: Penguin Collectors' Society (Miscellany 11), 1996

Powers, A., *Front Cover: Great Book Jacket and Cover Design*, London: Mitchell Beazley, 2001

Poynor, R., 'You Can Judge a Book by Its Cover', *Eye*, 39, spring 2001, pp. 10–11

——, *Typographica*, London: Laurence King, 2001

——, *Communicate: Independent British Graphic Design since the Sixties*, London: Laurence King, 2004

——, 'Penguin Crime', *Eye*, 53, autumn 2004, pp. 52–7

Schleger, P., *Zero: Hans Schleger, a Life of Design*, London: Lund Humphries, 2001

Schmoller, T., 'Roundel Trouble', *Matrix*, 14, pp. 167–77

Shaughnessy, A., 'An Open and Shut Case', *Design Week*, 26 April 2001

Spencer, H., 'Penguins on the March', *Typographica* (new series) 5, London: Lund Humphries, June 1962, pp. 12–33

——, 'Penguin Covers: A Correction', *Typographica* (new series) 6, London: Lund Humphries, December 1962, pp. 62–3

——, *Pioneers of Modern Typography*, London: Lund Humphries (1969), 1982

Ten Years of Penguins: 1935–1945, Harmondsworth: Penguin, 1945

Watson, S. J. M., 'Hans Schmoller and the Design of the One-Volume Pelican Shakespeare', *Typography Papers*, 3, University of Reading: Department of Typography & Graphic Communication, 1998, pp. 115–37

Williams, W. E., *The Penguin Story*, Harmondsworth: Penguin (Q21), 1956

Websites

www.penguin.co.uk
    The company's main website, with information about current titles, background information, and links to the various company divisions and worldwide sites.

www.pearson.com

The parent company's site, which contains information about the organization of the entire group.

www.penguincollectorssociety.org

The Penguin Collectors' Society site, containing much useful information, not least about their own publications, but also links to other sites. *The Penguin Collector* and its predecessor the *Newsletter* have been published twice yearly since 1974 and are a mine of information about all aspects of the company's history.

Archives

The Penguin Archive, including the collections of the papers of Allen Lane and Eunice Frost, company correspondence and editorial 'job bags', is housed at University of Bristol Information Services, Special Collections:

www.bris.ac.uk/is/services/specialcollections

The archive of Penguin Books itself is housed at the Pearson Group distribution centre in Rugby. It contains copies of virtually every title published. Enquiries to The Archive, Pearson Shared Services, Pearson Distribution Centre, Central Park, Rugby CV23 0WB.

Logo Development, 1935–2005

1. Penguin, 1935.

2. Puffin, 1968.

3. Penguin, 1946.

4. Puffin, 1941.

5. Allen Lane, 1967.

6. Penguin, 1946.

7. Porpoise, 1948.

8. Penguin, 1938.

9. King Penguin, 1948.

10. Puffin, 1940.

11. Pelican, 1948.

12. Penguin, 1947.

13. Penguin, 1949.

14. Penguin, 1950.

15. Puffin, 1941.

16. Penguin, *c.*1987.

17. Pelican, 1948.

18. Pelican, 1937.

19. Kestrel, 1970.

20. Penguin, 1948.

21. Penguin Education, 1967.

22. Puffin, *c.*1959.

23. Allen Lane, 2003.

24. Penguin, 1949.

25. Pelican History of Art, 1953.

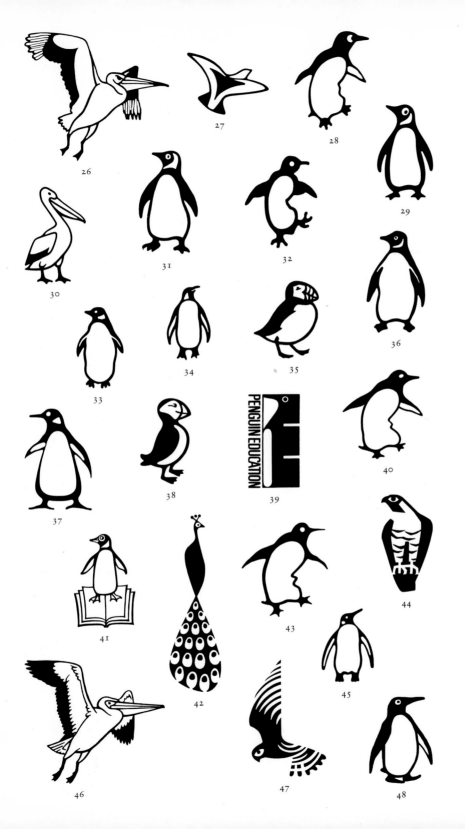

26. Pelican, 1937.

27. Ptarmigan, 1945.

28. Penguin, 1944.

29. Penguin, 2003.

30. Pelican, 1949.

31. Penguin, 1938.

32. Penguin, 1945.

33. Penguin, 1935.

34. King Penguin, 1948.

35. Puffin, 1948.

36. Penguin, 1948.

37. Penguin, 1947.

38. Puffin, 2003.

39. Penguin Education, 1967.

40. Penguin, 1945.

41. Penguin, 1947.

42. Peacock, *c.*1963.

43. Penguin, 1948.

44. Peregrine, 1962.

45. King Penguin, 1939.

46. Pelican, 1948.

47. Kestrel, 1970.

48. Penguin, 1937.

Index

To avoid excessive length, books are indexed only if they are referred to in the text or appear in more than one cover design; titles are indexed under their authors. Italic figures refer to illustrations.

Acknowledgements

The initial idea for this book came from Penguin Press designer David Pearson, to whom I owe the biggest thanks. While the words are mine, and the design his, the development of the book has been very much a collaborative effort which took place against a background of train and car journeys, late-night phone conversations and hundreds of unprintable email discussions.

Many people have helped with the book's progress during the past year. Friends: David Rose and Jonathan Pearson, Stuart Evans of Central Saint Martins. In my studio: Woojung Chun, Mala Hassett, Jack Schulze and Geoff Williamson, and I thank my other clients for their patience. At Penguin: Commissioning Editor Helen Conford; Sue Osborne, Lindsey Cunningham and Tina Tyler in the archive at Rugby; Antonio Colaço, John Hamilton, Tony Lacey, John Seaton and Jim Stoddart at 80 Strand. Past designers and editors of Penguin or its imprints: Derek Birdsall, Jerry Cinamon, Richard Hollis, Romek Marber, David Pelham and Dieter Pevsner, and Hans Schmoller's widow Tanya. Tim Graham and the Penguin Collectors' Society. Martin West. Hannah Lowery and Michael Richardson of the University of Bristol Library Special Collections.

My copy-editor Richard Duguid, Steve Hare of the Penguin Collectors' Society, and fellow typography teacher Catherine Dixon helped greatly at various stages of the writing process in clarifying and correcting the text. But any remaining errors, as they say, are mine.

My final thanks are to my family, Jackie, Beth and Felicity, who have had to tolerate both the inevitable disruption that writing a book brings to daily life and a massive influx of second-hand books (not to mention the shelves to accommodate them).

Picture credits

All books photographed are from the Penguin Archive in Rugby. The poster featured on p. 2 is courtesy of William Grimmond's family and the Penguin Collectors' Society. Artwork samples, author portraits and marginal photographs are from the Penguin Archive at the University of Bristol, except p. 14 (Old Style No. 2 and Times New Roman samples), David Pearson; p. 53 (John Curtis), courtesy the Estate of John Curtis; p. 96 (Arup and Dowson building), Phil Baines; p. 98 (Romek Marber), courtesy Romek Marber; p. 101 (David Pelham), courtesy Peter Williams; p. 102 (the Marber grid), courtesy Romek Marber; p. 162 (Derek Birdsall), courtesy Derek Birdsall; p. 222 (John Hamilton), courtesy John Hamilton; p. 223 (Jim Stoddart), courtesy Justine Stoddart; p. 224 (80 Strand), Phil Baines. The logos featured on pp. 250–51 have been scanned from book covers. Copystand photography by Carl Glover and David Pearson.